PRESENTED TO

....

BY

....

DATE

....

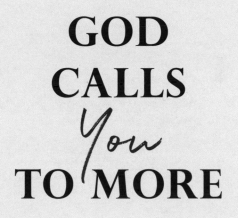

GOD
CALLS
You
TO MORE

GOD
CALLS
You
TO MORE

180 DEVOTIONS FOR MEN

BARBOUR
PUBLISHING

Editorial assistance by Elijah Adkins

ISBN 978-1-63609-596-7

Published by Barbour Publishing, Inc., 1810 Barbour Drive, Uhrichsville, Ohio 44683,
 www.barbourbooks.com

Our mission is to inspire the world with the life-changing message of the Bible.

Member of the
Evangelical Christian
Publishers Association

DON'T BE CONTENT TO COAST.
AIM HIGHER.
WORK HARDER.
DO MORE TO HONOR GOD.

Based on the familiar scripture 2 Timothy 2:15—"Do your best to present yourself to God as one approved" (NIV)—*God Calls You to More* is for every Christian man who knows there's more to life than ease and pleasure.

Each of these 180 readings encourages you to stretch yourself spiritually—not to earn your salvation but to honor the God who saved you.

On the pages to follow, you'll find all the familiar devotional book elements:

- a brief, memorable title
- an introductory scripture
- and a thought-provoking contemporary reading

But each entry is accompanied by a second page featuring:

- a relevant quotation
- practical suggestions or questions for further thought
- and a powerful prayer starter

God Calls You to More will challenge you to shake off complacency and work with God to change your world.

HOW MUCH IS "ENOUGH"?

*He who loves silver shall not be satisfied
with silver, nor he who loves abundance
with increase. This is also vanity.*

ECCLESIASTES 5:10

In the 1987 movie *Wall Street*, the aptly named character Gordon Gecko utters an oft-quoted line: "Greed, for lack of a better word, is good."

But the Bible would disagree. Greed, it teaches, is a destructive force in the life of any man—especially a man of God.

The apostle Paul wrote that "the love of money is the root of all evil" and that some who have an insatiable desire have "gone astray from the faith and pierced themselves through with many sorrows" (1 Timothy 6:10).

God is not against earning money—or even against accruing wealth—as long as we do it righteously. In fact, the Bible repeatedly encourages His people to work hard so that they may prosper. But what God is passionately against is letting money become your final goal—an idol that takes the place of your family and even God Himself. Money may be important, but relationships mean infinitely more.

So approach your work with passion. Work hard to provide well for yourself and your family. But never lose sight of the fact that your ultimate satisfaction, your ultimate source of all good things, is your heavenly Father.

*The problem with the rich young ruler wasn't that
he had money—but that his money had him.*
STEVE CAMPBELL

❯❯ FOR FURTHER THOUGHT:

How important is money to you?

❯❯ PRACTICAL APPLICATION:

Do you make sure to spend time with God and family
each day, or does your work occupy most of your attention at home?

---

*Father, shield me from my worst tendencies.
Show me how to balance my finances healthily
and without obsession. You call me to so much
more—help me realize my true potential.*

DO GOOD. . .
EVEN WHEN IT HURTS

Who is he that will harm you if you are followers
of what is good? But even if you suffer for
righteousness' sake, happy are you! "And do not
be afraid of their terror or be troubled."
1 Peter 3:13–14

Have you ever done everything you can to demonstrate godly love to someone, only to have that person repay you with evil words, attitudes, and actions? When faced with such situations—as everyone is at some point—many Christians are tempted to turn to God and protest, "It's just not fair!"

No, it's not fair when a Christian suffers for doing what is good in God's eyes. But today's verse gives a twofold assurance for such a situation. First, it promises that even if a man of God is persecuted for doing good, he needn't fear any lasting harm. Second, it promises that God sees his suffering and will find a way to bless him in the midst of it.

So don't let the fear of harm knock you off the path. God calls you to more. . .and He'll provide the means for you to achieve it! All you have to do is trust Him enough to keep doing what you know is right in His eyes.

When facing opposition you either become more
dedicated or more discouraged. It's your choice.
BILL WILSON

⇥ FOR FURTHER THOUGHT:

When have you felt persecuted for doing right?

⇥ PRACTICAL APPLICATION:

Practice responding to persecution with these three
steps: (1) thank God for the chance to bring honor
to His name, (2) pray for your enemies, and (3) keep
doing what you're doing!

Jesus, You endured the worst treatment this world
has to offer, but that didn't stop You from doing Your
Father's will. Grant me the endurance to stay on Your
path—I know that unimaginable blessings await.

ACT LIKE MEN

Watch, stand fast in the faith, act like men,
be strong. Let all your things be done with love.
1 Corinthians 16:13–14

The Greek word *andrizomai* is used only once in the New Testament. In 1 Corinthians 16:13, it is translated as the imperative statement, "Act like men."

No, Paul wasn't encouraging the believers of Corinth to behave in stereotypical fashion—acting macho, cheering on their favorite team, or belching loudly. Rather, the word *andrizomai* is more like a commanding officer's order to his soldiers: be courageous!

Interestingly, Paul follows up this command with a reminder to act in love. This is a profound juxtaposition. Prepare for war, but arm yourself with love.

Paul knew a believer's life is a battleground. We must watch out for invisible enemies, stand firm in our Savior's grace, and stay strong against temptations. We must act like men, courageously loving others when it feels more natural to fight. It's the only way to rise above the mediocrity of everyday life.

In the battles you face today, arm yourself with the Savior's love. . .and show the world what it really means to act like a man.

Courage: The inner commitment to pursue a
worthwhile goal without giving up hope.
GARY SMALLEY

⤳ FOR FURTHER THOUGHT:

How can a Christian man stand his ground and show
his love at the same time?

⤳ PRACTICAL APPLICATION:

How can you "act like a man" the next time someone
confronts you about your faith?

---

*Lord God, I don't want my testimony to get
lost in an ungodly reaction to life's trials.
Grant me equal doses of courage and love—
that's the only way I can be a true man.*

DOING WELL

If you fulfill the royal law according to the scripture,
"You shall love your neighbor as yourself," you do well.
JAMES 2:8

Sometimes, we wonder if we are doing enough for God. We think about Jesus' commandments and teachings and wonder if we are living "Christlike" lives.

A rich young ruler once came to Jesus and asked Him what he must do to be saved. Jesus' answer reflected the idea He always taught: there's nothing anyone can do to earn his way into heaven. After all, God certainly isn't impressed by our work. Instead, our walk with Jesus is about a real relationship. It is about loving Him and loving others as ourselves. Isn't it wonderful that we have a God of love?

As James 2:8 teaches, we are living as we should if we obey God's law to love one another. Of course, this isn't always easy. But the way we love the person we like the least is the way we love God the most.

It's easy to hate our enemies. But if we accept God's higher calling—if we see people through Jesus' eyes—we will certainly "do well."

Yes, we never touch the ocean of God's
love as much as when we love our enemies.
It is such a joy to accept forgiveness, but it is
almost a greater joy to give forgiveness.
CORRIE TEN BOOM

›› FOR FURTHER THOUGHT:

Why would God sometimes place disagreeable people
in our lives?

›› PRACTICAL APPLICATION:

What "enemies" has God allowed into your life? How
do you deal with these people?

Lord, I want to "do well" in Your eyes. I need
Your strength so that I can love the people
You've placed in my life. . .just as You love me.

WHAT AM I DOING WRONG?

"You have sown much and bring in little. You eat,
but you do not have enough. You drink, but you
are not filled with drink. You clothe yourselves,
but no one is warm. And he who earns wages
earns wages to put it into a bag with holes."

HAGGAI 1:6

Hard times don't always indicate you're doing something wrong. Read Job's story for confirmation of that truth.

But sometimes, difficulties *do* point to sin—or at least misplaced priorities—in our lives. Haggai's brief prophecy indicates that.

God's exiled people had returned to Jerusalem. They quickly improved their own homes but left God's temple in ruins. So the Lord not-so-gently defined their problem. "You looked for much, and behold, it came to little," He said. "And when you brought it home, I blew it away. Why? . . . Because of My house that is desolate, while every man runs to his own house" (Haggai 1:9).

When life is hard, it's not a bad idea to ask God, "What am I doing wrong?" If He shows you something specific, confess and change it. If there's nothing obvious, God may just be calling you toward a closer walk with Himself.

God has a meaning in each blow of
His chisel, each incision of His knife.
He knows the way that He takes.

F. B. MEYER

›› FOR FURTHER THOUGHT:

Can you think of any spiritual flaws that might be
making your life more difficult at the moment?

›› PRACTICAL APPLICATION:

Use each trial as an opportunity to search for ways to
improve your spiritual life, praying for God's wisdom
as you go.

Lord, thank You for always knowing what's best,
even on days when I doubt that truth. Help me turn
each trial into an opportunity to grow closer to You.

MOVING AT GOD'S SPEED

*At the commandment of the LORD the children of
Israel journeyed, and at the commandment of the
LORD they camped. As long as the cloud remained
on the tabernacle they rested in their tents. And
when the cloud remained a long time, for many
days on the tabernacle, then the children of Israel
kept the charge of the LORD and did not journey.*

NUMBERS 9:18–19

The Israelites recognized that they would experience God's
guidance, blessing, and protection only as they resolved to
move with the cloud. Though they longed to venture into
the promised land, they had to entrust themselves to God's
direction for their lives.

When is it hard for you to wait on God's timing? Have
you ever felt that you've rushed ahead without God's guidance, provision, or protection? It can be humbling to admit
that we don't know what's best for ourselves. But remember
the lesson of Israel's story: moving forward without God's
power and leadership is far worse. Without God's trans-
forming presence in your life, difficult days are guaranteed.

For you, perhaps waiting for the Lord looks like seeking the counsel of someone at church or relinquishing your
desires for a particular outcome, knowing that God's plans
are so much greater. The delay may be agonizing, but God's
presence is worth waiting for.

Let me no more from out Thy presence go,
but keep me waiting watchful for Thy will—
even while I do it, waiting watchful still.
GEORGE MacDONALD

❖ FOR FURTHER THOUGHT:

Have you ever tried jumping ahead of God. . .only to find out that you've fallen several steps behind?

❖ PRACTICAL APPLICATION:

How can you train yourself to keep pace with God's plans?

Lord, thank You for walking ahead of me. Grant
me the patience and humility to follow in Your
footsteps instead of trying to make my own.

HONESTY WITH GOD

"I believe; help my unbelief."
MARK 9:24

The words spoken in today's scripture came from the mouth of a man who was out of options. Having heard of this man who had healed many sick, lame, and demoniacs, the man wanted Jesus to heal his demon-possessed son. But still, he doubted.

How could someone who had heard so much about Jesus possibly doubt Him? Isn't his reply a contradiction in itself? Surprisingly, no. Maybe the man had no problem believing Jesus could heal people. Maybe his words were instead an admission of his doubt that Jesus could (or would) help *him*.

Being this honest with God can be frightening. We all have things we wish we could hide from Him—things we don't even want to admit to ourselves. But when we come to the end of ourselves and still need God to do something great for us, He doesn't want our lip service. He wants us to say what we really feel—whether we like it or not. When we're brutally honest, God works best.

Do you sometimes find yourself doubting that God wants to do a miracle for you? If so, confess your doubt to Him. He can handle it. He can also open your heart and mind to the greater life He has planned for you.

Many of us mistakenly believe that God doesn't want us to be honest about our lives. We think that He will be upset with us if we tell Him how we really feel. But the scriptures tell us that God does not want us to be superficial in our relationship with Him, with others, or in our own lives.
ROBERT MCGEE

❯ FOR FURTHER THOUGHT:

Are there any lingering doubts and insecurities that you're afraid to confess to God?

❯ PRACTICAL APPLICATION:

Identify your doubts and put them into words. Then tell God about them, trusting Him to help you work through those questions.

Father, I know that with You, no confession is off-limits. Thank You for removing my shame whenever I speak honestly with You.

STOP YOUR GRIPING!

*Do all things without murmurings and
arguments, that you may be blameless and
harmless, the sons of God, without rebuke,
in the midst of a crooked and perverse nation.*

PHILIPPIANS 2:14–15

Let's face it—life can sometimes feel like one frustrating situation after another. Who among us, when circumstances put the squeeze on, hasn't felt like griping and complaining to anyone who will listen?

While the Bible contains some examples of good men who complained to God (David and Job, for example), it also warns us against grumbling—and shows us the negative consequences that come from having a complaining attitude (see Numbers 14).

When we complain, we separate ourselves from God and His peace. After all, it's hard to live up to God's plan for our lives when we're trudging every second of the way. But it also ruins our testimony for Christ to a lost and hurting world. Who'd want to listen to someone's answers when that person constantly grumbles about his own life?

So whenever you think life is unfair, remember to do as the apostle Paul instructed: "Give thanks in everything, for this is the will of God in Christ Jesus concerning you" (1 Thessalonians 5:18). Also remember God's promise that "all things work together for good for those who love God, for those who are called according to His purpose" (Romans 8:28).

*Those who choose complaining as their
lifestyle will spend their lifetime in the
wilderness. Complaining is sin.*
JAMES MACDONALD

›› FOR FURTHER THOUGHT:

How might your act of complaining hinder someone
else from accepting the gospel?

›› PRACTICAL APPLICATION:

Who in your life might be influenced by your choice to
either complain or show gratitude?

---

*Father, help me obey You with joy and gladness—
not with a scowl and grumbling. I want everyone
to know how amazing it is to follow You.*

GOD CALLS YOU TO REJOICE

Rejoice in the Lord always, and again I say, rejoice.
PHILIPPIANS 4:4

Paul wrote the words of today's scripture from prison. Considering his circumstances, it doesn't seem like he had much reason to rejoice. Yet he knew what many of us forget: when we have the Lord on our side, that's the only reason we need.

Paul didn't say, "Rejoice in your circumstances." He told us to rejoice *in the Lord.* When we're feeling depressed, anxious, or hopeless, we can think of our Lord. We can remind ourselves how unique and beloved we are to God. In His heart, each of us is irreplaceable.

Perhaps the reason we sometimes lose our joy is because we've entrusted it to the wrong things. If our joy is tethered to our finances, jobs, or relationships, what happens when those things fall through? Our joy sinks with them.

But thankfully, God has a better plan. When He is the source of our joy, we will never lose it. Circumstances may frustrate us and break our hearts, but God is able to supply all our needs. He is able to restore broken relationships. He can give us a new job or help us succeed at our current one. Through it all, we can rejoice, knowing that we are God's and that He loves us.

Christians without joy are basically useless to
the work of God. They will enter heaven when
they die, but they will take no one with them.
After all, who would want what they have?
JOE BEAM

❯❯ FOR FURTHER THOUGHT:

When trials arise, what's your typical reaction—anger
and frustration, or joy and peace?

❯❯ PRACTICAL APPLICATION:

Whenever you lose something—big or small—stop
to count your blessings and think on God's goodness
before you react.

It doesn't matter what trials come my way, God—
I know You're with me, and that's all the
reason I need to rejoice. Thank You for
Your comforting presence.

YOUR MISSION

He brought out His people with joy,
and His chosen with gladness.
Psalm 105:43

How dull the movies would be if every agent had the same
mission—and how predictable the outcomes. When it comes
to "impossible" tasks, there is something inspiring about
variety.

The same is true in real life. No two individuals have
identical assignments. Your task, should you choose to
accept it, is vital.

The Bible presents multiple examples of this. First
Chronicles mentions "the ruler of the house of God" (9:11).
Others were "very able men for the work of the service of the
house of God" (9:13). Each family accepted their mission,
and some fulfilled their mission over multiple generations.

In the book of Acts, Paul and Barnabas were appointed
(15:2) to go talk with the other apostles about whether new
believers needed to follow Old Testament requirements.
They accepted their mission.

The result of accepting and completing a mission is the
happiness and fulfillment that only God can give. After all,
only God can make your impossible mission possible.

No one is too messed up for God to use, and no task is too unimportant to matter to God.
STEPHEN ARTERBURN AND JACK FELTON

✦ FOR FURTHER THOUGHT:

How does watching God tackle your "impossible" missions compare to taking the easy way around?

✦ PRACTICAL APPLICATION:

What impossible tasks might God be calling you to pursue right now?

Almighty God, I want to keep my eyes and ears open for Your calling—even if the magnitude of it seems absurd. Give me the faith I need to take the plunge.

IT'S NEVER TOO LATE TO REPENT

"'Because your heart was tender and you have humbled yourself before the LORD when you heard what I spoke against this place and against its inhabitants, that they should become a desolation and a curse, and you have torn your clothes and wept before Me, I also have heard you,' says the LORD."
2 KINGS 22:19

Although Josiah feared disaster because of God's judgment, he took prompt action to acknowledge his people's sins and to grieve the ways in which they had angered God. The Lord was eager to hear such prayers, and He relented from His anger immediately.

We all fail, sometimes in dramatic and even public ways. You may worry about letting people down with your poor choices. You may think you're a phony. However, you can't "outsin" God's love and concern. Even the most stubborn sinners found rich mercy and forgiveness when they changed their ways. Jesus went so far as to suggest that God throws a party for one repentant sinner!

Today is the day to examine your failure, shame, and weakness, and to bring them to God. There is nothing beyond His mercy. . .and if you trust Him with your paths, you can change how you see yourself. The good news is that God has never changed the way *He* sees you. You are always a beloved child who will be readily welcomed home.

Why stay stuck in shame and guilt when God calls you to more?

*Do not linger in the shame of sin as if
such suffering will bring in holiness.*
WATCHMAN NEE

» FOR FURTHER THOUGHT:

Do you tend to wallow in guilt over sin, or are you
quick to confess to God and move on?

» PRACTICAL APPLICATION:

Make a habit of confessing your sins right away and
thanking God for His mercy.

*Lord, I thank You for second chances. I want
to constantly improve in my walk with You,
so help me never to become stuck in the past.*

GOD CALLS YOU TO SIMPLICITY

John [the Baptist] had his clothing of camel's
hair and a leather belt around his loins,
and his food was locusts and wild honey.
MATTHEW 3:4

From the wilderness of Judea, John the Baptist appeared preaching about the kingdom of heaven. Everything about him pointed to a rough, outdoorsy lifestyle—from his plain style of clothing to the food he ate. Many people probably expected the Messiah's forerunner to arrive with more pomp and circumstance. But that wasn't the case.

John's simple lifestyle allowed him to focus solely on the kingdom. One Bible commentator suggests that John was so consumed with spiritual things that he couldn't even find time for a set meal. So quick snacks of locusts and wild honey were just fine.

It's easy to become overwhelmed by lengthy to-do lists. But time spent with God is absolutely essential to our well-being. Whether you escape to a quiet corner of the house or make an actual wilderness getaway, take some time to be alone with God. Embrace simplicity—and listen for His voice.

*One of the rewards of following Christ is the
simplicity and wonder it brings to life.*
JOSEPH STOWELL

❯❯ FOR FURTHER THOUGHT:

How often do you spend "alone time" with God?

❯❯ PRACTICAL APPLICATION:

Try thinking of items in your busy schedule that you
can give up in order to prioritize your spiritual health.

---

*Lord, I want to be like John—so concerned
about following You that everything
else feels trivial. Show me how to bring
simplicity into my walk with You.*

TRUE TO YOUR INNER CONVICTIONS

And Paul, earnestly looking at the council,
said, "Men and brothers, I have lived in all
good conscience before God until this day."
ACTS 23:1

After his arrest, Paul—a Jew and Roman citizen—stood before the Sanhedrin and chief priests to plead his case. With a clear and good conscience, the apostle declared his commitment to God, his fervent determination to serve and please Him, and his faultless life even before his conversion to Christ.

Before Jesus, Paul lived according to the Jewish law and ordinances and remained true to those teachings. He was void of hypocrisy or dishonesty and acted from his conscience. After Paul's conversion, he was a warrior of faith resolute to serve the Lord with all holiness and zeal, ever mindful of his call to God and service to others.

The word *conscience* comes from a Latin word that means "what one knows with oneself." The conscience is the inner faculty that decides the moral quality of our thoughts, words, and actions. Our consciences are seared with remorse when we do wrong and endowed with peace and satisfaction when we choose right. All of us must live with our own consciences, whether good or bad.

In another passage Paul said, "And in this I exercise myself to always have a conscience void of offense toward God and toward men" (Acts 24:16). May we all do likewise!

Conscience is God present in man.
VICTOR HUGO

❖ FOR FURTHER THOUGHT:

How does God work within our human consciences to align our own ideas of right and wrong with His?

❖ PRACTICAL APPLICATION:

When was the last time you felt God working through your conscience to change your attitude about a situation? How did you respond?

Father, help me follow my conscience. And if there's anything in my conscience that needs correcting, reveal it to me. I want my actions to align with the commands in Your Word.

LETTING GO

And he left the oxen and ran after Elijah,
and said, "Let me, I ask you, kiss my father
and my mother, and then I will follow you."
1 Kings 19:20

When the prophet Elijah threw his mantle over Elisha's shoulders, he made Elisha his successor. But Elisha's first reaction was to go home and say goodbye to his parents. He had trouble letting go.

His reaction reminds us of those who made excuses for not following Jesus. In His parable of the great banquet (Luke 14:15–23), Jesus recounted three kinds of things people have trouble releasing.

The first man bought land and needed to see it. He couldn't let go of his *place*.

The second man bought oxen and had to see them. He couldn't let go of his *possessions*.

The third man wanted to be with his new wife. He couldn't let go of *people*.

Both Elisha and the characters in Christ's parable had the opportunity for a new life and a tremendous adventure. But their stories end very differently.

Elisha went back, slaughtered his oxen, burned the plow, and (we assume) bade farewell to his parents. He severed the ties to his past and went after his future (1 Kings 19:21).

The characters in Jesus' parable clung to their place, possessions, and people. They wouldn't let go. They lost the opportunity, missed the feast, and watched others enjoy what could have been theirs.

When God calls us to take up our cross and follow Him, the first thing we must have is empty hands (Mark 8:34–38).

Jesus is trying to get us to understand a key dynamic principle. When we give up our tight grasp on our own life, we discover life as it was meant to be lived.
GREG LAURIE

❯ FOR FURTHER THOUGHT:

When has God called you to give something up—a hobby, possession, or even relationship—to draw closer to Him?

❯ PRACTICAL APPLICATION:

Practice obeying God each time you feel His leading on a moment by moment basis. That way, it'll be easier to obey Him when big decisions must be made.

Father, I want You to be the focal point of my life. May I never grow so attached to something in this world that I wouldn't be willing to give it up at Your command.

READ YOUR BIBLE!

Your word is a lamp to my feet and a light to my path.
PSALM 119:105

Life is busy, isn't it? We spend eight-plus hours a day, five-plus days a week working, and then we have to make time for family, friends, church, and church-related activities. Sometimes, we're squeezed for time, and one of the first casualties is our time alone with God in prayer and Bible reading.

The writer of today's scripture understood that God's Word gives believers direction. It lights their way. But the apostle Paul went even further: "All scripture is given by inspiration of God and is profitable for doctrine, for reproof, for correction, for instruction in righteousness, that the man of God may be perfect, thoroughly furnished for all good works" (2 Timothy 3:16–17).

So the words recorded in scripture lead and guide us, teach us, rebuke and correct us, and show us what it means to be righteous. Can there be any question as to how important our time in God's Word is?

Reading books and other material about the Bible is a good thing. Attending group Bible studies is probably even better. But God calls you to go beyond the superficial: He wants you to spend time *alone with Him*, meditating on His written Word.

It is not the quantity that is read, but the manner of reading, that yields us profit.
FRANÇOIS FÉNELON AND JEANNE GUYON

✦ FOR FURTHER THOUGHT:

On average, how much time each day do you spend studying God's Word?

✦ PRACTICAL APPLICATION:

Today, start a journal chronicling how much time you spend in Bible study, what you learned, and how you can apply those truths to your life.

God, thank You for the priceless treasure that is Your Word. I want to use it to learn more about You each day so that I can fulfill Your calling for my life.

DON'T TRUST YOUR MONEY

Charge those who are rich in this world not to be
haughty or trust in uncertain riches but to trust in the
living God, who richly gives us all things to enjoy.
1 TIMOTHY 6:17

It's easy to default to trusting in money. After all, cash seems to solve problems, resolve anxieties, create friends, and generally make people happy. But there's a harsh reality behind this rosy picture.

Paul taught that money is unreliable. . .and our own experience confirms his words. Recessions wipe out billions of dollars of savings overnight. Banks collapse. Financial institutions fold. Solomon warned, "Riches certainly make themselves wings; they fly away like an eagle toward heaven" (Proverbs 23:5).

If you have money, good for you. Chances are that you worked hard or smart (or both) to earn it. But you still shouldn't put too much trust in it. That's tantamount to trusting in yourself, and Deuteronomy 8:18 says, "you shall remember the LORD your God, for it is He who gives you power to get wealth." God is a surer foundation than money could ever be. Only He can supply everything you need. . .including such priceless qualities as love, faith, peace, and assurance before Him.

When you serve God, you are using God's money to
accomplish His wishes. But when you serve money,
you are using God's money to accomplish your wishes.
Bruce Wilkinson

✦ FOR FURTHER THOUGHT:

Judging by your decisions and attitudes, which do you trust more: God or money?

✦ PRACTICAL APPLICATION:

How can you learn to set your mind on things above?

Father, I know You have given me everything
I own. I don't want to prioritize my blessings
over the one who gave them to me. Help
me use my wealth to do Your will.

REPLACE THE VOICES

Now we have received not the spirit of the world but the Spirit who is from God, that we might know the things that are freely given to us by God.

1 CORINTHIANS 2:12

Ancient Greece placed a high value on worldly wisdom and philosophy. That's what makes Paul's statement in today's scripture really stand out. Then as now, if Christians wanted to understand the things of God, they couldn't rely on what the world around them offered. Instead, they needed to look to the Holy Spirit.

Today, we aren't tempted to emulate Greek philosophers—or even to look them up, probably. But how often have we listened intently to self-help motivational speakers whose advice subtly elevates personal desires over the biblical principle of dying to ourselves?

God's calling may not be the easiest path, but Christian men soon learn that it is infinitely better than the flimsy, feel-good way of life that the world offers.

Once you identify those false messages, quickly replace them with godly voices who will help you understand and rely on the Holy Spirit. This doesn't take special training. Just quiet your heart and open the Word—then listen for the Spirit's voice.

*Any philosophy that makes it
easier to sin is of the devil.*
VANCE HAVNER

⇢ FOR FURTHER THOUGHT:

How often do you hear opinions that contradict the Bible?

⇢ PRACTICAL APPLICATION:

Today, pay close attention to every opinion and topic of discussion that you hear. See what does and does not align with the Bible, using specific verses to back up your conclusions. Then consider how you can integrate this practice into your everyday life.

---

*Lord, I know You're the only one who always
tells the truth. Help me never to place more
stock in worldly wisdom than in Your Word.
Show me how to discern truth from error.*

NO ONE SAID IT WOULD BE EASY

And He has made alive you who
were dead in trespasses and sins.
EPHESIANS 2:1

Anyone who says it's easy to reach spiritual maturity is a liar. Anyone who *believes* it's easy is a fool.

The Bible writer James said we should rejoice in trials because of what they produce in us (James 1:2–4). The apostle Paul compared this life to the harsh discipline of an athlete in training (1 Corinthians 9:24–27). Jesus warned us that we would have trouble in this world (John 16:33). And the Bible compares our spiritual journey to gold ore in the refiner's fire (Proverbs 17:3) or clay on the potter's wheel (Jeremiah 18:1–5).

When we pursue Jesus Christ with all our hearts, our lives will challenge the world around us. . .and may prompt angry, hostile responses. Since the world hates Him—and all who follow Him—spiritual warfare is inevitable. Our enemy will use all his power and influence to deceive us, block our way, and make sure we pay a high price for following God.

But we have an even more formidable enemy: ourselves. We run from, resist, and resent the struggles we inevitably face. Too often, we want the glory without the cross. But it never, *ever* happens that way.

No one said it would be easy. . .just worth it!

*Those whom God uses most effectively have
been hammered, filed, and tempered in
the furnace of trials and heartache.*
CHARLES SWINDOLL

❯ FOR FURTHER THOUGHT:

What people or circumstances in your life try to
dissuade you from your spiritual walk? How effective
are they?

❯ PRACTICAL APPLICATION:

How can you turn any bitterness and fatigue you
might be feeling into determination?

---

*Father, thank You for the trials I'm facing. I can't say
that I enjoy them when they come, but I know You
always have a greater reason for letting them happen.*

BEWARE CARELESS WORDS

*"Not so with My servant Moses, who is faithful in
all My house. I will speak with him mouth to mouth,
even clearly, and not in dark speeches, and he shall
behold the form of the LORD. Why then were you
not afraid to speak against My servant Moses?"*

NUMBERS 12:7–8

Miriam and Aaron had spoken against Moses, criticizing his
Cushite wife and claiming that they had the same authority
to speak on God's behalf. The Lord's judgment put an end to
both of their claims against Moses, offering a reminder that
careless words and criticisms can lead to heavy consequences.

Far from giving every leader immunity from criticism,
this passage warns against our desire to think more highly
of ourselves or to unjustly attack a person in authority. Even
more, it shows that careless criticism rarely yields positive
results. Rather, our careless words can lead to division in the
community and a strong diminishment of our own reputation.

By the time God was finished exposing the pride of
Aaron and Miriam, they had no illusions about themselves.
Before speaking up, consider whether you may be blinded
by your own illusions. Have you considered yourself more
qualified or connected to God than someone else? If so,
proceed cautiously.

Although we cannot all be writers,
we all want to be critics.
MARTIN LUTHER

❯❯ FOR FURTHER THOUGHT:

Why is it so easy to criticize others in the same areas
that we offer excuses for ourselves?

❯❯ PRACTICAL APPLICATION:

What steps are you taking to break this pattern of
thinking?

Lord God, I sometimes get frustrated and resort
to placing blame on others, even when they
are innocent. Help me to live by Your higher
standard, not by my own double standards.

LOOK UP!

Therefore, I will look to the LORD. I will wait for the God of my salvation. My God will hear me.
MICAH 7:7

Few people had harder lives than God's prophets. They carried tough messages to tough people—and often experienced tough results.

Take Micah, for instance. Though he made the beautiful prediction of Jesus' birth in Bethlehem (Micah 5:2), he was soon saying, "Woe is me! . . . The good man has perished from the earth, and there is no one upright among men. They all lie in wait for blood. Every man hunts his brother with a net. . . . The son dishonors the father, the daughter rises up against her mother, the daughter-in-law against her mother-in-law. A man's enemies are the men of his own house" (Micah 7:1–2, 6).

In such a fallen world, Micah could only look up toward God's higher purpose. What would that accomplish? "When I fall, I shall arise," he said. "When I sit in darkness, the LORD shall be a light for me" (Micah 7:8).

Despair can open the heart to taste hope in God.
DAN ALLENDER AND TREMPER LONGMAN III

❯❯ FOR FURTHER THOUGHT:

Are you often plagued by feelings of hopelessness? How long do these emotions last?

❯❯ PRACTICAL APPLICATION:

What are some ways you can train your mind to look beyond circumstances and toward God's calling?

Father, help me to have Micah's mindset.
When I'm blindsided by sickness, tragedy,
financial loss, or doubts, show me how to look up.
You're the only constant in this world of chaos.

HIDE THE WORD IN YOUR HEART

Your word have I hidden in my heart,
that I might not sin against You.

PSALM 119:11

We hide things for two reasons. We are either ashamed of something or we treasure it so much that we hide it for fear of someone stealing it from us.

David knew great sin, but he also knew great forgiveness. In his experience, hiding the Word of God in his heart was the only way to combat his sinful nature and keep him from falling even further.

To "hide" the Word in your heart implies several things. First, it means more than simply owning a copy of God's Word. Owning a book changes nothing. Second, it means more than hiding the Word in your mind. Your memories can fail you. Third, it means more than reading God's Word on occasion. Reading it is helpful. But possessing it in your heart is transformative.

If you find your faith lacking the power to overcome sin, consider starting a Bible memory program. It doesn't have to be elaborate. Index cards will work just fine. Look up verses that address the sin you are struggling with and jot the verses down on the cards. Carry them with you everywhere and refer to them throughout the day.

If you study, meditate on, and recite the verses often enough, they'll soon be hidden in your heart—the perfect place for the Holy Spirit to access them for your spiritual breakthrough.

Labor to remember what you read. Satan would steal the word out of our mind; not that he intends to make use of it himself, but lest we should make use of it.
THOMAS WATSON AND SAMUEL LEE

⇥ FOR FURTHER THOUGHT:

How many Bible verses have you committed to memory?

⇥ PRACTICAL APPLICATION:

Look up some go-to verses for whenever temptation, worry, or doubt strikes. Commit to memorizing them.

God, I know Your Word is more than just a decoration on my bookshelf. Show me how to integrate it into every aspect of my life, even when I don't have a copy of scripture on hand.

WHEN AN ENEMY FALLS

*Do not rejoice when your enemy falls, and do
not let your heart be glad when he stumbles,
lest the LORD see it, and it displease Him,
and He turn away His wrath from him.*

PROVERBS 24:17–18

Schadenfreude is a German word for feeling pleasure or joy at the troubles or failures of another person. While there may not be an exact English equivalent for this word, it's safe to say that the emotion itself is universal.

Have you ever felt at least a small twinge of satisfaction when someone you know—say a competitor in business or a person who treated you unfairly—fell on difficult times? If so, then you should know that God calls you to a higher standard.

Jesus instructed His followers to pray for their enemies and adversaries, not to wish ill on them—and *certainly* not to rejoice at their downfall (Matthew 5:44). When you walk in obedience to this command, in effect you're saying, "God is bigger than any conflict I have with another person, and I'm going to trust Him enough to respond to that person's suffering in a way that pleases Him."

*There is no mystery about it. We love
others, we love everybody, we love our
enemies, because He first loved us.*
HENRY DRUMMOND

✦ FOR FURTHER THOUGHT:

Imagine what the world would be like if everyone—
even sworn enemies—helped each other in times of
need.

✦ PRACTICAL APPLICATION:

Brainstorm some ways you can bring the world one
step closer to this ideal today.

---

*Father, I know You take no pleasure in judging
others. Help me not to take pleasure in it either.
Rather, help me love people in the midst of
their struggles, pointing them to Your love.*

AVOID ARGUMENTS

But avoid foolish and ignorant questions,
knowing that they breed strife. And the
servant of the Lord must not quarrel but be
gentle to all men, able to teach, patient.
2 TIMOTHY 2:23–24

If you're tempted to get drawn into arguments, you might not see it as a fault. You may simply think that you're being honest, "telling it like it is," or setting other people straight. But the fact is, most quarrels generate far more heat than light—and end up creating hard feelings. They often descend into emotional shootouts rather than reasoned discussions. This is especially true of political and religious arguments—as well as many marital disagreements.

Ask yourself what you spend the most time doing during a typical argument. Are you patiently listening to the other side, trying to understand that person's point of view, or does "listening" mean impatiently waiting for your turn to speak? The Bible calls God's servants to be "gentle listeners." Does this describe you?

Granted, there are times, especially when someone is teaching dangerous false doctrine, when you must "earnestly contend for the faith" (Jude 3). But with God's help you must rise above your emotions, contending with facts and solid reasons, not with a raised voice and intimidating body postures.

Solomon said, "The beginning of strife is like when one

lets out water; therefore, leave off contention, before it is meddled with" (Proverbs 17:14). Know what's actually worth disputing and what's not. Whether you feel you're right or not, the wisest thing that you can do is often to simply avoid getting drawn into an argument in the first place.

If you want to stop an argument, close your mouth.
CHARLES SWINDOLL

❯❯ FOR FURTHER THOUGHT:

Which is more important to you: winning a victory in an argument, or preserving a friendship?

❯❯ PRACTICAL APPLICATION:

The next time you're in the middle of a brewing conflict, ask yourself, "What will this argument gain?" If the answer is "nothing," break away immediately and give yourself time to cool off.

All-knowing God, teach me how to be
levelheaded when it comes to disagreements.
I don't want any angry words to fly from
my mouth and stain my witness for You.

SPIRITUAL PROSPERITY

*Better is the poor who walks in his integrity than
he who is perverse in his lips and is a fool.*

PROVERBS 19:1

The man who walks in his integrity is satisfied at the end of
the day. He's finished an honest day's work, treated people
well, and comes home to a quaint but satisfying meal. He
has nothing to be ashamed of. He's put forth his best effort,
and tomorrow is another day.

The man who is crooked, however, is foolish. He speaks
lies and cuts corners to get ahead. He mistreats people for his
own gain. He dines extravagantly and drives fancy vehicles,
in hopes of impressing others. His conscience bothers him
from time to time, but he rationalizes his actions, telling
himself that everybody does wrong things. He covers up his
sins and falls asleep scheming about the next day.

Which of these men do you think is living up to God's
calling?

Not surprisingly, the Hebrew word for *integrity* in today's
verse can be translated as "prosperity." In other words, the first
man, even though he has less money, is far more prosperous
than the second man could ever dream.

In the economy laid out by Proverbs 19:1, there is no
middle class. Which side of the spectrum are you on?

God only, and not wealth, maintains the world;
riches merely make people proud and lazy.
MARTIN LUTHER

❯ FOR FURTHER THOUGHT:

Why do you think the world's standard of rich and
poor is often exactly the opposite of God's?

❯ PRACTICAL APPLICATION:

Are you actively trying each day to value heaven's
rewards more than earth's?

Lord, I don't care if the world says I'm poor.
As long as I have You, I'm the richest man alive!
Thank You for giving me a purpose that's so
much higher than mere fame and fortune.

YOU GROW BY
BECOMING CHILDLIKE

*"Truly I say to you, whoever shall not
receive the kingdom of God as a little
child shall in no way enter it."*
Luke 18:17

Jesus holds up children as the best teachers about the kingdom of God. What is it about children that makes them
so qualified? Perhaps their simple dependence and trust in
their parents can show us what it's like to live in the freedom
of God's realm.

Many adults who grew up in poverty report similar
experiences: in most cases, they'll note that during their
childhood, they "never knew" they were poor, and that
their parents found ways to make ends meet. Even in some
of the most heart-rending cases, children found contentment
and confidence in their parents. Many times, a loving and
present parent was more than enough to compensate for
life's challenges.

Today, whether you're secure or in great need, a childlike
dependence on God is where you'll find long-term comfort
and contentment. Growth in wisdom or maturity certainly
has its place. However, Jesus also expects you to grow more
"childlike" if you're going to truly live in His kingdom.

*To be a blessing to our children, we simply need
to become childlike ourselves—to believe God's
call and to receive God's grace for the task.*
JACK HAYFORD

❯ FOR FURTHER THOUGHT:

What is your heart filled with the most—a child's trust
or a cynical adult's skepticism?

❯ PRACTICAL APPLICATION:

Pay attention to the small children in your life—
whether they're your own or someone else's. See how
they respond to their parents' reassurances, even in the
direst of situations.

---

*Father, please give me a childlike faith.
I'm tired of being cynical and skeptical—
show me how to approach each situation
with an unwavering trust in Your goodness.*

PICK YOUR BATTLES

As for these four children, God gave them knowledge
and skill in all learning and wisdom. And Daniel
had understanding in all visions and dreams.
DANIEL 1:17

Daniel was one of the first Hebrew exiles taken from Jerusalem into "friendly" captivity in Babylon. When he was separated from his family, forced into servitude, and given a new identity and new gods, Daniel was probably only a teenager. He was now living in Babylon, the pagan center of the earth.

Did Daniel completely reject his new lifestyle? Did he argue with his master and refuse to learn? No. Amazingly, there were only a few areas where Daniel refused to compromise: he would not bow down to any other god or eat food that had been offered to idols.

We live in a type of Babylon too. We're surrounded by anti-God behavior, customs, and culture. It's easy to be offended by just about. . .everything. Conversation is flavored with swear words, television shows mock our faith, and schools introduce curricula that make us cringe.

Surprisingly, God didn't tackle every single issue in Babylon. Instead, He picked Daniel's battles for him, using this young man greatly in the midst of a pagan culture. Daniel wasn't indignant or antagonistic—he was compassionate and sought the best for his captors.

Can we be Daniels in our communities today?

Simply put, we need churches that are self-consciously distinct from the culture. We need churches in which the key indicator of success is not evident results but persevering biblical faithfulness.
MARK DEVER

❯ FOR FURTHER THOUGHT:

Are you passively influenced by your culture, or do you strive to influence it?

❯ PRACTICAL APPLICATION:

How can you fulfill God's greater calling by thoughtfully engaging with unbelievers?

It's sometimes just as tempting, Lord, to shut my eyes and ears to my culture as it is to passively absorb its values. Help me to do neither. Show me instead how to use my interactions with the culture to make an impact for You.

A HOPE BEYOND THE PRESENT

"'For I know the thoughts that I think toward you,' says the Lord, 'thoughts of peace and not of evil, to give you an expected end.'"

JEREMIAH 29:11

Can you trust that God has wonderful plans for you—that He desires to give you a future and a hope? It would seem that *everyone* would embrace such a promise, but many find it difficult to do so. They're focused on the world's problems—pollution, poverty, pandemics, economic crises, weather conditions—and think it's too late for hope.

If you read only the dismal headlines, it's easy to develop a negative mindset. Things *are* becoming more difficult. But in the midst of all this, God calls you to a life of faith and hope, not fear. He says, "I have spoken these things to you, that in Me you might have peace. In the world you shall have tribulation, but be of good cheer: I have overcome the world" (John 16:33).

When Jeremiah prophesied hope, the Jews also had little reason to have any—God was still punishing them for their sins. However, He wanted His people to look beyond the present and trust Him for a wonderful future. He wants you to do the same.

God, who foresaw your tribulation,
has specially armed you to go through it,
not without pain but without stain.
C. S. LEWIS

❯ FOR FURTHER THOUGHT:

How has God used tribulation to accomplish His purposes throughout history?

❯ PRACTICAL APPLICATION:

How might God be using your current problems to achieve a greater good?

Father, thank You for offering hope—a way
to rise above life's day-to-day uncertainty.
I know that no matter what happens, I can
have peace by resting on Your promises.

ASK GOD FIRST

David inquired of God, saying, "Shall I go up
against the Philistines? And will You deliver
them into my hand?" And the LORD said to him,
"Go up, for I will deliver them into your hand."
1 CHRONICLES 14:10

Men of action sometimes see prayer as a last resort, but men of faith ask God first. King David learned this the hard way in the previous chapter of 1 Chronicles. Over the next few chapters, David asked God first before taking any action.

The first two times, David prayed about whether to attack the raiding Philistines. The first time, God said, "Go." The second time, however, God gave much different instructions. David never could have dreamed up those instructions. He needed to hear from God.

The third time David prayed, the Lord reminded him that He'd already given detailed written instructions to Moses on how to transport the ark. No one else needed to risk suffering the terrible consequences of disobeying God. . .like Uzza did in 1 Chronicles 13:10. Instead, God's people celebrated with all their might.

"Ask God first" isn't just a meaningless platitude—it's actually a vitally important strategy for fulfilling His higher calling for your life.

Ask God first *plus* listen to God *plus* obey God *equals* success.

The devil often laughs when we work,
but he trembles when we pray.
CORRIE TEN BOOM

⁂ FOR FURTHER THOUGHT:

When difficult situations arise, what is your knee-jerk reaction?

⁂ PRACTICAL APPLICATION:

How can you train yourself to pray first and then listen for God's answer before you address a problem?

Lord God, give me the wisdom to seek You
in prayer, the patience to wait for Your reply,
and the courage to obey whatever command You give.

CALLED TO DEPENDENCE

*"This is the word of the L*ORD *to Zerubbabel,*
saying, 'Not by might, nor by power, but
*by My Spirit,' says the L*ORD *of hosts."*
ZECHARIAH 4:6

Men tend to admire the self-reliant, independent types—those who seem able to solve any problem and accomplish any task without outside help. Here in the West, that attitude is called "rugged individualism."

There's no question God can use such a man to accomplish great things for His eternal kingdom. However, that can only happen when this man humbles himself and learns to trust not his own abilities but the empowerment of the Holy Spirit.

Zerubbabel led the first wave of Jewish exiles returning to their homeland from the Babylonian Exile. God had charged him to lead in the rebuilding of His temple, which had been destroyed decades earlier. He had also provided him with some very able men to accomplish this huge task. Still, God let them know they wouldn't complete the assignment through their own strength but only through His empowerment.

God isn't interested in sharing His glory with anyone. Instead, He calls His men to rely completely on Him in all areas of their lives. So if you want to accomplish something for God's kingdom, never forget that you can only do it by His Spirit.

*The essential thing in Christian living is not
where you are going or what you are doing,
but in whose strength you are living.*
GEORGE VERWER

❯❯ FOR FURTHER THOUGHT:

When you accomplish something great, what emotions
spring up first in your mind—pride or thankfulness?

❯❯ PRACTICAL APPLICATION:

Try shifting the focus from yourself and onto God in
your workplace, family life, and pastimes.

---

*Father, I know You're the source of my every
breath—I can do nothing without You. Remind
me of this each time pride tries to arise inside me.
May every good deed I do point to You alone.*

FALL TO RISE

The proud looks of man shall be humbled,
and the haughtiness of men shall be bowed down.
And the LORD alone shall be exalted in that day.

ISAIAH 2:11

Have you ever been forced to spend time around a proud, boastful man? You know, the kind who never seems to have anything to say unless it's about himself and his accomplishments?

Being around that kind of man for any length of time can be draining. Pride is a sin each man struggles with in one way or another. But most men, even the ones who let pride run unchecked in their own hearts, find it repulsive in others.

Just think, though: how much more repulsive does God—who lists humility as a high virtue—find our pride? So much so that He tells us, "God resists the proud but gives grace to the humble" (James 4:6).

James's use of the word *resists* carries with it an ominous meaning. It connotes a God who doesn't just let the prideful man go about his way but who actively works against him.

Pride is a serious sin that leads nowhere good. That's why God calls you to a life of humility. "Humble yourselves therefore under the mighty hand of God," the Bible says, "that He may exalt you in due time" (1 Peter 5:6).

Throughout our time on this earth, and in every arena of our lives, you and I share a common greatest enemy: pride.

C. J. Mahaney

❯ FOR FURTHER THOUGHT:

Why do you think God hates pride more than most other sins?

❯ PRACTICAL APPLICATION:

What steps are you taking to combat pride in your own life?

Lord, You're the only one who deserves glory. Teach me greater humility and help me resist the urge to boast. I want to be a walking testimony to Your greatness.

GLORYING IN TRIBULATION

And not only so, but we also glory in tribulations,
knowing that tribulation works patience,
and patience experience, and experience hope.
ROMANS 5:3–4

The man who has been justified by faith has peace with God through the Lord Jesus Christ (Romans 5:1). He glories not only in the hope found in Christ but in tribulation. That sets him far apart from the man who hasn't been justified by faith and is devastated when tribulation comes.

Consider your last tribulation. Maybe it was an illness, a job loss, or an injury. Maybe it was something more severe, like the loss of your home or a family member. After mourning your loss, how did you respond? Did you see the spiritual benefit in it?

It isn't that God wants you to be happy about your loss; rather, He wants your loss to transform and shape your character. And ultimately, He calls you to an eternal hope through temporal pain.

Trust Jesus Christ to use your deepest heartache for the advancement of His kingdom in you. Lean on Him and show the world the true power of the gospel.

*Be thankful for the providence which has made
you poor, or sick, or sad; for by all this Jesus works
the life of your spirit and turns you to Himself.*
CHARLES SPURGEON

⤖ FOR FURTHER THOUGHT:

Can gratitude sometimes be harder to offer in times of
peace? Why or why not?

⤖ PRACTICAL APPLICATION:

Practice being thankful for the tiny things, even when
life is going smoothly. Then, whenever trials arrive,
gratitude will come more naturally than bitterness.

---

*Lord, thank You for working steadfastly to draw
me to You. Train my eyes to see life from Your
vantage point and not from my own perspective.*

SILENCE AND REST

*LORD, my heart is not haughty or my eyes lofty,
nor do I exercise myself in great matters or in
things too high for me. Surely I have behaved
and quieted myself, like a child who is weaned by
his mother; my soul is even as a weaned child.*

PSALM 131:1–2

Perhaps you have a "tough love" picture of the Lord, seeing Him as a God who demands much of you. If so, today's psalm reminds you that God nurtures and cares for you the way that a mother cares for her child.

If you miss this truth, you may well become proud of your holiness, your commitment to God, or your spiritual accomplishments. You may attempt to master "great matters" that distinguish you from others. The pride that comes with performing for God will inevitably result in haughty glances at others. You imagine that they either don't measure up or are a threat to your own pursuit of (a false) holiness.

However, if you see God as infinitely loving like a mother caring for a child, you can respond to Him with silence and rest. Your striving will cease, giving way to total trust in His protection and acceptance.

Only by being humble and caring for others—knowing you have nothing to prove or to guard—can you live up to God's grand calling.

*The fruit of the Spirit was never intended to be
a demonstration of our dedication and resolve.
It is the evidence of our dependency on and
sensitivity to the promptings of the Spirit.*
CHARLES STANLEY

✧ FOR FURTHER THOUGHT:

Why do you think God values dependence
over independence when it comes to our relationship
with Him?

✧ PRACTICAL APPLICATION:

How can you turn a desire for independence into a
passion for dependence—on God alone?

---

*Father, I know that on my own, I'm a mess.
That's why I need Your Spirit to direct my
actions and mold my heart. I simply can't
make it without Your intervention.*

CALLED TO COOPERATE

The ants are a people not strong, yet they
prepare their food in the summer.
PROVERBS 30:25

Ants have something going for them that we people don't: they lack selfishness. Their teamwork can be seen all over the world.

In some climates, ants make their nests and tunnels entirely underground. But in areas where clay soils drain poorly, they build hills out of leaf stems, evergreen tree needles, and sand. They carry each tiny item from wherever they find it on their travels.

The hill makes a nest and tunnel system that rises above puddles of rain and mud. It also repels the drops that fall on its domed top. As weather permits, the industrious ants enlarge and maintain their hill. And even when moss and grass overtake those hills, their unmistakable shape remains.

Wherever they live, ants cooperate to gather food. They seem to function as if the entire colony were controlled by one mind.

What a picture for us as believers, to work together as if we are controlled by one mind—the mind of Christ!

*The church needs both unity and diversity
if it is to function in this world.*
WARREN WIERSBE

❖ FOR FURTHER THOUGHT:

What ministries are you actively involved in at your
local church?

❖ PRACTICAL APPLICATION:

Find ways to cooperate with other believers in order
to advance God's kingdom—mission trips, community
volunteer projects, etc.

---

*Thank You, God, for placing so many fellow believers
in my life. There's nothing quite like the feeling of
working alongside others to achieve a common goal.
Help me never to take this blessing for granted.*

BE WILLING

*Now therefore fulfill doing it, that as there was a
readiness to be willing to do it, so also there may be a
fulfillment out of what you have. For if there is first a
willing mind, it is accepted according to what a man
has, and not according to what he does not have.*

2 CORINTHIANS 8:11–12

Sometimes, the only ability we bring to a task is our willingness.

In today's scripture, the apostle Paul urged the Christians of Corinth to complete a job: namely, the collection of a financial gift for poor believers in Jerusalem. The Corinthians had been willing, even eager, to be part of the relief effort, but they apparently needed some apostolic cheerleading to finish the job. Paul implored them not to give up but to keep doing the good works they were called to do.

At the time Paul wrote, the Corinthians had plenty. They could give generously to the Christians at Jerusalem and expect equivalent treatment if they ever found themselves in similar straits (verse 14). But more important than their resources was the Corinthians' willingness to help. The apostle noted that their attitude made the gift acceptable to God.

God doesn't call everyone to wealth. . .but He calls *all* of us to be willing. And when we are, God accepts our efforts based on what we have, not what we lack.

I do not believe one can settle how much
we ought to give. I am afraid the only safe
rule is to give more than we can spare.
C. S. Lewis

✦ FOR FURTHER THOUGHT:

Are you willing to give? If so, how do you express that willingness each day?

✦ PRACTICAL APPLICATION:

What strategies did Paul use to convince the Corinthians of their need to be generous? How might we incorporate some of these strategies in our approach to evangelism?

Lord Jesus, You were willing to give everything—
even Your life—for my sake. Please grant me
the willingness to give to others as well.

MAKING HIS WAYS YOUR ROUTINE

And his master saw that the LORD was
with him and that the LORD made all
that he did to prosper in his hand.

GENESIS 39:3

Joseph's story is a classic riches-to-rags-to-riches tale, but the most remarkable thing about him—his greatest trait—was that God was with him. This fact explains Joseph's survival, his successes, and the wise and compassionate character he consistently showed.

God calls you to make Him the core of *your* daily routine. It takes discipline not to take God for granted, to seek Him when things are going well and not just when they aren't. Joseph's consistency made him a model employee—the best worker his bosses had, a conduit of God's blessings to them. Joseph's success had nothing to do with his education or accomplishments and everything to do with his trust in God.

God is faithful, even when you're not. That's not a guilt trip but a "get out of jail" card—a gift that can't be earned, only received. And you can tell that you have received it, not because all the storms in your life suddenly cease but because you suddenly have a remarkable sense of peace and freedom as you face them.

We will never have pure hearts unless we do whatever it takes to consistently get ourselves into the presence of God.
ANGELA THOMAS

❖ FOR FURTHER THOUGHT:

How can you improve your trust in God for tomorrow?

❖ PRACTICAL APPLICATION:

Today, write down each problem you face as well as your response. Next, before you go to sleep, review the list and see how consistently you trusted in God throughout the day.

God, I know You call me to so much more than a simple reliance on my own efforts. Show me how to increase my dependence on You—that's the only way true freedom can be found.

LIFE IS SHORT—CHOOSE GOD

For what is your life? It is even a vapor, that
appears for a little time and then vanishes away.
JAMES 4:14

At the end of your life, you don't get a mulligan, do-over, or divine reset. You have one life to make the right decisions and determine your place in eternity. Your time on earth isn't an end game, it's a potent beginning. If you only live for what you can get here, you're missing out on the preparation for what's to come.

Life is like grass—here for a season and gone. Life is like fog—visible and impactful for a short period of time. Life is shorter than you realize, yet long enough that you're sometimes convinced to put off making the decisions that must be made today.

You can choose to do things your own way, or you can find out what God wants you to do. You can determine your own "truth," or you can consult the God of all truth. You can live as though this life is all there is, or you can discover this life is a small step into forever.

The only redeemable promises and guarantees you have in life are *God-made*. He promises to be with you. He calls you to rise above temporal pleasures and pursue an eternal life with Him. There's no good reason to intentionally separate yourself from God. Life is short, so choose Him.

Human beings are in desperate need of salvation. Time is short, God's wrath is certain, and eternity hangs in the balance.
ALBERT MOHLER JR.

❯ FOR FURTHER THOUGHT:

Why do you think God arranged this world so that everything here eventually wears out or dies?

❯ PRACTICAL APPLICATION:

Judging by your actions alone, how much do you value eternity? What changes might be appropriate in your thinking?

Father, thank You for the days You've given me. Help me never to waste my time chasing useless things that will crumble into nothingness the moment I die. I want my pursuits to be everlasting.

THE REWARD WILL COME

And let us not be weary in doing good, for in
due season we shall reap, if we do not faint.
GALATIANS 6:9

Don't let anybody fool you: the Christian life is tough. If it weren't, why would the apostle Paul write what he did in Galatians 6:9?

Well doing often comes with weariness. It sometimes leads to moments when we feel like fainting—or giving up, as newer translations of the Bible say. In today's verse, Paul was describing the difficulties of restoring a fellow Christian who's fallen into sin. We are called to carry each other's burden to fulfill the law of Christ (verse 2). But we must beware of the danger of falling into sin ourselves, perhaps by thinking we are better than our sinning brother (verses 1, 4).

Another well-known passage describes sowing and reaping, spiritually speaking: "Do not be deceived; God is not mocked, for whatever a man sows, that he shall also reap" (verse 7). It's all work! Sowing, reaping, restoring fellow believers who stumble. . .

The good news is in verse 9, where Paul—speaking for God—promises a harvest for those who answer the call to this hard yet fulfilling life. But we can't faint, and we don't dare give up.

Stay on task, do your work faithfully, allow God to provide the strength. . .and then wait for the reward. It will come.

We are called to endure and not grow
weary or give up, but to hold fast.
BENEDICT OF NURSIA

❯❯ FOR FURTHER THOUGHT:

When was the last time you grew tired of doing good?
What decisions did you make in that moment of
weakness? Do you have any regrets?

❯❯ PRACTICAL APPLICATION:

How might the reminder of past failures strengthen
your resolve for the next trial?

Lord, I'm glad You didn't give up on the way
to the cross. Show me how to have the same
level of determination in everything I do—
no matter how weak and tired I become.

WISE WORDS

"But let your communication be 'Yes, yes' or 'No, no.'
For whatever is more than these comes from evil."
MATTHEW 5:37

Part of being trustworthy is being a man of your word. It's a lost value in an age where almost everyone feels like lying is sometimes the best route. In a broken world, you must look to God as your anchor for what is true and right. To be a man of your word, you must first be a man of God's Word.

God's living Word cuts through the world's shifting morality and offers clarity (Hebrews 4:12). Even when an issue isn't specifically addressed, the Bible directs you to timeless principles that not only guide you but offer you a brighter path forward. It doesn't matter if, in the world's eyes, God's way is narrower and more challenging.

James wrote, "But you be doers of the word and not hearers only, deceiving your own selves" (James 1:22). A man for whom God's Word is his bond will stand out. When people ask you why you are like you are, you can tell them it's because you're trusting your words to God, who called you to a higher standard and helps you live up to it.

*Honesty is like a flu shot. It may give you a short,
sharp pain, but it keeps you healthier in the long run.*
WILLARD HARLEY JR.

❯❯ FOR FURTHER THOUGHT:

Are you friends with anyone who stays unflinchingly
honest, even when it's hard? If so, what's your opinion
of this person?

❯❯ PRACTICAL APPLICATION:

Using the same standards you applied to your friend,
how honest are you? What changes might be appropriate in your thoughts, words, or actions?

---

*God, I want to live by the standards set forth
in Your Word. . .and that includes being honest.
Give me the courage to stand up for the truth,
even when I feel nobody wants to hear it.*

REACH FOR THE JOY

*Through much tribulation we must
enter into the kingdom of God.*
ACTS 14:22 NIV

Mountain climbers get a unique feeling when they step onto a summit they never thought they'd reach. Bicyclists get the same sensation when they push through exhaustion to a refreshing downhill slope. Sailors feel the joy when they pass through the discomforts of being cold and wet to become one with the wind.

We've all had our own version of that incredible feeling. You know when and how it happened, but the words to describe it probably failed you. These are the moments we rise above this world and briefly touch a joy beyond our understanding.

Always remember that heaven will be far better than even our most exhilarating moments on this earth. Don't you think that's worth any hardships we face now?

It is easy to be religious when religion is in fashion; but it is an evidence of strong faith and resolution to swim against a stream to heaven, and to appear for God when no one else appears for him.
MATTHEW HENRY

❯ FOR FURTHER THOUGHT:

How do the small victories of this world compare to the joys that heaven will bring?

❯ PRACTICAL APPLICATION:

This week, record each moment of triumph you experience. Then ask yourself, "What did it take to reach this point?"

Heavenly Father, I don't want to focus on the pain of the here and now. I know You've called me to a purposeful life and given me a hope that overshadows every trial. Thank You.

OVER AND ABOVE

Now to Him who is able to do exceedingly abundantly above all that we ask or think, according to the power that works in us, to Him be glory in the church by Christ Jesus.

Ephesians 3:20–21

This scripture concludes Paul's prayer for the Ephesian church for spiritual growth, inner strength, and knowledge of God's love (verses 14–19). The passage is a doxology, a hymn of praise to God and assurance to every believer of the omnipotence of our loving Lord.

The apostle declares that God is able to do "exceedingly abundantly." The Greek word *huperekperissou* has a rare double compound meaning. It means God is not only able to accomplish all things, but He does so "superabundantly above the greatest abundance"—or "beyond measure."

"Above all that we ask or think" is just that. Imagine every good thing that God has promised in His Word—or things you've only dreamed about. Think of wonderful things that exceed the limits of human comprehension or description, and then imagine that God is able—and *willing*—to do even more!

The last part of this verse indicates that the Holy Spirit works within the Christian's life to accomplish the seemingly impossible. Our highest aspirations are within God's power—but like Paul, we must pray. When we do, God does far more for us than we could ever guess.

New life, supernatural life, the abundant life of
the living Christ is imparted to the person who
in desperation turns from the old, barren, bleak
ways of the world to keep company with Christ.
W. Phillip Keller

» FOR FURTHER THOUGHT:

What do you feel when you think of a joy that can't
be comprehended in this life—but which you will
one day know? Excitement? Longing? Curiosity?
A mixture of all?

» PRACTICAL APPLICATION:

For perspective when life feels mundane or frustrating, focus on the grand mysteries that surround God's
character. Then remind yourself that you will one day
see Him face-to-face!

Lord, I sometimes try to imagine what awaits me
in heaven, but each time, I come up short. Help
me continue living for You so that this speculation
and mystery will one day give way to sight.

CALLED TO CONTENTMENT

Whom have I in heaven but You? And there
is none on earth that I desire besides You. My
flesh and my heart fail, but God is the strength
of my heart and my portion forever.

PSALM 73:25–26

Desire in and of itself can be good and healthy, but how often do we suffer grief or disappointment because we have desired the wrong thing? Maybe we think of such desires as coming from the enemy, pulling us away from God.

God doesn't delight in thwarting or stifling your desires. If you've grown up with a long list of religious rules to follow, hearing that may be a shock. However, no one has ever found God by amassing a list of things to do and stopping there. The psalms take us one step further.

Today's psalm invites you to rethink your desires—asking where your desires are directed. Are they toward temporary things, or are they directed toward something higher—the God who passionately loves you and who would love to affirm your true self in union with Him?

There are a thousand ways to be discontented, lonely, and disappointed. But there's only one way to find the love and acceptance that you've been craving since day one. There's no need for a thousand paths—God's love has always been yours as long as you seek His presence!

You can be sure that your deepest desires reveal
important truths about your spiritual condition.
Tullian Tchividjian

❯ FOR FURTHER THOUGHT:

Where do your true desires lie? Are there any repeated
sins in your life that might indicate they're not where
they should be?

❯ PRACTICAL APPLICATION:

If you find a specific issue that you struggle with, get to
the root of the problem by asking God to change your
desires. Once your desires change, so will your habits.

Thank You, Lord, for offering true satisfaction.
Help me never seek any sort of substitute—I know
none of them will compare to the real thing.

AS YOU MAKE YOUR PLANS. . .

Commit your works to the LORD and
your thoughts shall be established.

PROVERBS 16:3

If you've ever been involved in planning for a project or new campaign at work, you know there's one all-important step to take before any plans can become reality: your manager or boss needs to sign off. Without their approval, serious problems await.

The same thing can be said for the Christian who wants to launch out into some kind of new ministry or professional or personal endeavor. In today's scripture, Solomon offers a great bit of wisdom when it comes to planning. The best kind of planning, he says, starts with committing your vision to your ultimate boss—your heavenly Father—and continues as you allow Him to give ongoing direction.

Many lofty plans—even those that seemed appointed by God—have failed because those with the vision didn't first submit their work to the Lord. After all, you can't fulfill God's plan if you refuse to let it override your own.

Planning is the bedrock of all important things you do. It's simply not a good idea to undertake a new endeavor without it. So by all means, plan. But as you make your plans, don't forget to submit them to God for His approval and direction.

*Don't forget to consider the spiritual side of your life
when planning for any new season of your life.*
KEN OWEN

❯ FOR FURTHER THOUGHT:

Why do you think God doesn't allow us glimpses into
the future?

❯ PRACTICAL APPLICATION:

Does your inability to see the future bolster your
reliance on His plans, or does it lead to increased
anxiety? Talk with God about how you can best
respond to the twists and turns of life.

---

*Eternal God, help me never to be foolish
enough to make plans without Your approval.
You're the only one who knows the future and
who can lead me in the best direction.*

DO YOUR PART

*Then He shall give the rain for your seed that you
shall sow in the ground and bread from the increase
of the earth, and it shall be rich and abundant.*

ISAIAH 30:23

Most Christians know that God is all-powerful.

We realize that He provides the soil and weather conditions to make crops flourish. But He could also easily plant the seeds, irrigate them, and root out the weeds. He could simply drop food from heaven, as on rare occasions He's chosen to do. But generally speaking, farmers and gardeners have to sow their seeds, care for the plants, and take in the harvest. From there, human effort turns the raw material into the foods we enjoy.

We are totally dependent upon God for our food—but human beings are also completely involved in the process.

That's a striking picture of the Christian life. God supplies all the power. We just have to walk in it. If we don't do our part, our spiritual lives wither and die. But if we do, God grows rich and plentiful spiritual fruit into us.

Labor is God's education.
RALPH WALDO EMERSON

❯ FOR FURTHER THOUGHT:

Are you currently praying for someone else who
has a need? Is it possible that *you* might be the best
candidate to answer that prayer?

❯ PRACTICAL APPLICATION:

How can you blend prayer and action when it comes
to meeting someone else's needs?

---

*Father, thank You for giving me the chance to
work for You—and the strength to do it. Help me
take advantage of this strength every opportunity
I get. I want my prayer to have hands and feet.*

WORTH REACHING OUT

He was despised and rejected by men,
a man of sorrows and acquainted with grief.
And we hid, as it were, our faces from Him.
He was despised, and we did not esteem Him.

Isaiah 53:3

Several hundred years before Jesus' birth, the prophet Isaiah predicted that Christ would take on the sins of the world for our salvation.

The description of this man—as someone we'd rather not look at, a man bent under the burden of sin—might apply to lots of people in the world today. We probably all know people we don't like talking to: nasty, evil, or just plain unpleasant people. But they weren't meant to be like that! Sins—theirs and others'—have twisted their lives.

They didn't take that burden on board for us, and they certainly didn't do it for our salvation. But that doesn't mean we should look away. We tend to do so, however, because we fear if we reach out to them, they might bring us down. People certainly felt the same about Jesus.

But within each person, there's a soul that God loves and wants to find. That's why He calls us to reach out to them in His name. Who knows—it might just result in their salvation.

What do you see in the stare of a stranger?
Christ's love compels us to reach across barriers.
STEPHEN MOSLEY

✦ FOR FURTHER THOUGHT:

Is there someone whom you see every day but never speak to—maybe another guy at work, a homeless man by the street, etc.?

✦ PRACTICAL APPLICATION:

Think of ways you can enter that person's world— a kind word, a little bit of assistance, or even an attempted friendship.

Lord God, thank You for not ignoring me when I was a sinner. Show me ways to be there for others—even the people I don't want to associate with. I want to shine Your light in their lives.

FAITHFUL IS SUCCESSFUL

Study to be quiet, and to do your own business,
and to work with your own hands.
1 Thessalonians 4:11

In the parable of the talents (Matthew 25:14–30), Jesus told of three men who were given money, "every man according to his separate ability" (Matthew 25:15). The first two doubled their investment, but the third held onto his money and was condemned for doing nothing with it. This story reveals a few things about God's definition of success.

First, success comes when you've done the work in front of you—the work God has "before ordained" for you to do (Ephesians 2:10). Next, it means that God hasn't assigned everyone the same type of work or given everyone the same resources. But it also means that whatever He has given you is enough for you to do your job. So no matter what you do for a living, do it to honor God.

No amount of money can increase God's kingdom. But one man—whether he's digging ditches or investing stocks—can make the difference for the people he's working with, building the eternal nation one person at a time. When you're focused on answering God's high call, attending to "your own business" takes on a fresh attitude—you're minding *God's* business. In His view, faithfulness equals success.

A successful life is lived by one who has the right priorities in his life—being obedient to God's Word—and then putting into action what he knows to be true.
BOB AND EMILIE BARNES

❯ FOR FURTHER THOUGHT:

What talents has God given you? What activities do you enjoy doing?

❯ PRACTICAL APPLICATION:

Think of ways you can use the talents and pleasures of your life to advance God's kingdom.

Thank You, Lord, for giving me a set of abilities and desires. Please show me how to use these gifts to give You the maximum amount of glory.

CONFIDENCE TO LIVE GOD'S WAY

And [Jehoshaphat's] heart was lifted
up in the ways of the LORD.
2 CHRONICLES 17:6

"Fake it until you make it" may be a popular slogan, but it's terrible advice. Granted, it's meant to shore up self-confidence in a world that works overtime to put you down.

During which times in your life did you feel the most confidence? Perhaps it was as a student, musician, athlete, artist, actor, techie, or collector. Perhaps it was your first promotion or big win in the work world. What stole that confidence? Was it something you did or failed to do? Or something someone said or did to you?

Consider what God has to say to you: "My son, how much I love you! There is nothing you could do to make Me love you more. . .or less. I created you, planned your days, adopted you into My family forever, and now indwell you. I want to fill, lead, guide, empower, and bless you!"

God calls you to hear Him, trust Him, and allow Him to work in and through you. Like good King Jehoshaphat, you can enjoy great confidence to live the way God wants you to live.

Receive that confidence today.

God will often use the desert of quiet faithful service, or the prison of injustice, to permanently transform our self-confidence into Christ-confidence. It is only when control is out of our own hands and we are thrust blindly into God's arms that He is free to teach us that He can be completely relied upon.
TIM BURNS

❖ FOR FURTHER THOUGHT:

What methods does the devil use to steal a Christian's confidence?

❖ PRACTICAL APPLICATION:

What are your strategies in fighting against those schemes? How well do they line up with those given in the Bible?

Father God, on my own, I have no reason to be confident about anything. Thank You for giving me solid ground on which to rest my assurances. I know Your promises will never fail.

JUDGE NOT

*There is one Lawgiver, who is able to save and
to destroy. Who are you who judges another?*

JAMES 4:12

Have you ever "gotten even" with someone? Have you ever reacted unkindly to someone else's unkindness? We've all done it. It's our way of passing judgment. We think people deserve it, so we give it to them.

That kind of judgment never makes us better people. That's why God calls us to choose a better alternative: love. Love isn't just a "soft" option—the option that gets you taken advantage of and that makes you look like a fool. In fact, think of how foolish you look when you sink to your enemies' level just because "they deserve it." That's just a win-win situation for the devil.

Jesus clearly taught us to love God and one another. It's the answer to every problem, and anyone who dismisses it obviously hasn't tried it. Judging others usually only garners a harsh judgment in return. Don't judge—love. Then when it comes our time to face the Lawgiver, His judgment on you will be a love you don't deserve.

You can't get ahead if you're trying to get even.
L. James Harvey

» FOR FURTHER THOUGHT:

When was the last time you resisted the urge to get even? How did that make you feel in the long run?

» PRACTICAL APPLICATION:

Practice the art of letting go the next time someone treats you badly. You can pray to God for His strength.

Lord, I sometimes want to get revenge on people who treat me wrongly. But that's when I remember the sacrifice You made for sinners like me. Help me show the same degree of mercy.

CALLED TO BLESS

*"Now give me wisdom and knowledge, that I
may go out and come in before this people,
for who can judge this great people of Yours?"*

2 CHRONICLES 1:10

Out of everything Solomon could have asked of God, he
sought something that would bring the most benefit to the
people he ruled. Given a chance to receive a blessing from
God, he sought a way to bless others.

Perhaps one way to think about your spiritual growth
today is to seek ways you can grow in your ability to bless
others. Rather than seeking financial security just for yourself,
ask God to grow your generosity so that you can help others
become secure. Rather than asking for safety for yourself
alone, ask God to show you people in your community who
are vulnerable. As you seek to bless others richly, you may
find that God takes care of your needs as well.

If you are facing a seemingly insurmountable challenge,
now is a great time to lean on God, trusting in His provision.
Turning your focus toward the ways you can bless others—
rather than the ways you may fail—can increase your faith
in God's provision.

We never outgrow our need for others.
In fact, giving ourselves to help others is
even more life building than receiving help
from others. The law of living is giving.
GEORGE SWEETING

❯ FOR FURTHER THOUGHT:

Do you know anyone in your community, church, or workplace who needs help of some kind?

❯ PRACTICAL APPLICATION:

How can you draw from your own resources today in order to be the answer to someone else's prayer?

God, I have a lot of needs, but I know that everyone else does too. Show me how I can meet the needs of others before worrying about my own.

SEVEN THOUSAND REASONS

*[Elijah said,] "Lord, they have killed Your prophets
and dug down Your altars, and I alone am left,
and they are seeking my life[.]" But what
is God's answer to him? "I have reserved for
Myself seven thousand men who have not
bowed the knee to the image of Baal."*

ROMANS 11:3–4

In 1 Kings 18, the prophet Elijah challenged 450 priests of Baal to a showdown of epic proportions. With all Israel watching, Elijah called down fire from heaven, devouring a massive, water-soaked offering in divine fashion. The people fell on their faces, confessing God, then dispatched the pagan priests. Furious, Queen Jezebel swore to kill Elijah. He ran away, hid in a cave, and—completely discouraged—poured out his complaint to God.

How did God encourage Elijah during his spiritual depression? By reminding him of the anonymous men who had resisted the pressure of their times—ordinary men who were faithful day after day. Elijah may have been the star of this epic, but these unknown men were the story behind the story. Through their witness, God encouraged one of the most powerful prophets of the Bible.

Few of us will ever know anyone who faces the pressures Elijah did, but we all know someone who feels alone in standing for God. That was Lot's experience in Sodom: "For that righteous man, dwelling among them, vexed his righteous soul from day to day in seeing and hearing their unlawful deeds" (2 Peter 2:8). Just remember, in a faithless world, all it takes to be an encouragement to others is to be one of the seven thousand.

I have come to believe strongly that people can never be encouraged too much.
Hans Finzel

» FOR FURTHER THOUGHT:

Make a list of the times you were influenced by someone else's godly example.

» PRACTICAL APPLICATION:

Think of someone (or multiple people) who could use the same kind of encouragement from you. Then reach out.

Lord, I want to live a godly life—not just for my own sake but for the sake of everyone who might see me. Teach me how to exemplify Your righteousness.

SOME NEEDED SELF-AWARENESS

But the other, answering, rebuked him, saying,
"Do you not fear God, seeing you are in the
same condemnation? And we indeed justly,
for we receive the due reward of our deeds.
But this man has done nothing wrong."

LUKE 23:40–41

In the most pivotal moment in all human history, the Creator of the world hung nailed to a wooden cross between two criminals. One mocked Jesus, and the other—painfully aware that he was receiving his just punishment—spoke the words recorded above.

Then a true miracle happened. This admitted criminal turned to the Lord and said, "Lord, remember me when You come into Your kingdom" (Luke 23:42). The Savior answered, "Truly I say to you, today you shall be with Me in paradise" (23:43).

The criminal's words hold a universal truth: "We [are punished] indeed justly, for we receive the due reward of our deeds." Every man deserves God's judgment and punishment. That's the bad news.

The good news is that when you recognize your unworthiness for God's eternal kingdom, you can place your faith in the one who died and rose from the dead. One day, you too will be with Him in paradise.

All Christians are forgiven an unpayable debt,
not because we deserve it, not as a reward
for doing penance by which we somehow
pay for our own sins, but solely on the basis
of what God Himself has done for us.
JOHN MACARTHUR

❖ FOR FURTHER THOUGHT:

Why do you think many people reject God's offer of salvation and instead try to earn it themselves?

❖ PRACTICAL APPLICATION:

Take a moment each day to remember the time God saved you. Reflect on how His grace overcame your sin. . .and use that memory to glorify Him in your heart continually.

God, I know I can do nothing to earn Your
love. Help me never to think my salvation
stems from my own goodness. Remind me of
my own sinfulness and of Your great grace.

DO I HAVE TO, LORD?

"Lie on your left side and lay the iniquity of the house of Israel on it; you shall bear their iniquity according to the number of the days that you shall lie on it. For I have laid on you the years of their iniquity; according to the number of the days."

 EZEKIEL 4:4–5

Ever get restless under God's commands? Even as Christians, we struggle with temptation. We often want to do our own thing and avoid what He says.

Imagine being Ezekiel. God told him to act out the upcoming siege of Jerusalem. The prophet was to build a little model of the city and then lay down beside it for 430 days—390 on his left side and 40 on his right—to indicate the years of Israel and Judah's sin. Ezekiel would be on public display for well over a year. *Really, God?*

Our Christian life is a paradox—God calls us out of sin and into a life of servitude. Just remember: any sinful pleasures we choose to pursue may very well destroy us. But anything we give up for God will be richly rewarded, in this life or the next. . .or both.

Growth in God comes by obedience...
perpetual obedience.
STEVE SAMPSON

❖ FOR FURTHER THOUGHT:

According to the Bible, what sort of rewards does God have waiting for those who serve Him?

❖ PRACTICAL APPLICATION:

The next time you're on the fence about whether to obey God, remind yourself of the life (and ultimate death) God has rescued you from.

God, I don't always understand Your methods.
Sometimes, I'm tempted to disobey You and do
things my own way. But because You know
everything, I surrender today to Your leading.

LIVE AS GOD'S CHILD,
NOT HIS SLAVE

And because you are sons, God has sent forth the
Spirit of His Son into your hearts, crying, "Abba,
Father!" Therefore, you are no more a servant but a
son, and if a son, then an heir of God through Christ.
GALATIANS 4:6–7

The Christian life is meant to be lived as a child of God, seeking the Spirit's confirmation of God's presence and acceptance. If you are seeking to obey God out of duty or fear, you've unintentionally demoted yourself from child to servant in His eyes.

Consider the voices in your heart today. Are they telling you that you aren't good enough for God or that God is angry at you? If those voices aren't calling out "Abba, Father," then you can rest assured they aren't from God.

Today is an invitation to be reoriented by the Holy Spirit. Every other priority, possession, and goal in life pales in comparison to the inheritance of peace and joy you've been promised in Christ as an heir in God's family.

This inheritance is yours if you are willing to seek the Spirit's voice in your life. Gladly accept your new identity as a beloved child of God the Father today.

The opposite of a slave is not a free man. It's a worshipper. The one who is most free is the one who turns the work of his hands into sacrament, into offering. All he makes and all he does are gifts from God, through God, and to God.

MARK BUCHANAN

⇾ FOR FURTHER THOUGHT:

Regularly check your heart to see if your motivations for obeying God are still pure.

⇾ PRACTICAL APPLICATION:

To ensure your motives spring from love and not obligation, look up verses that speak of how God feels about His children. Then imagine Him personally encouraging you with these words.

Father, I don't want to serve You out of mere obligation. May I be filled with joy at the thought of walking where You lead. Remind me of the immense freedom that Your love brings.

CALLED TO ACT

*And when He had spoken these things, while they
watched, He was taken up, and a cloud received
Him out of their sight. And while they looked
steadfastly toward heaven as He went up, behold,
two men stood by them in white apparel, who also
said, "Men of Galilee, why do you stand gazing up
into heaven? This same Jesus, who has been taken
up from you to heaven, shall so come in similar
manner as you have seen Him go into heaven."*

ACTS 1:9–11

After Jesus' work on earth was over, He ascended into heaven.
The disciples watched Him leave, staring up into the sky
even after He was completely out of sight, perhaps hoping
for another glimpse. Eventually, God had to send two angels
to tell them to move. Their apprenticeship was over. It was
time to do the work their Lord had called them to do.

When God tells us to work, we may be tempted to
stand still and continue to look for absolutely clarity. How
often do we hope that God will give us more instruction or
make our pathway absolutely certain? But the apostle Paul
has written, "We walk by faith, not by sight" (2 Corinthians
5:7). In other words, as followers of Christ, we move through
life one faithful step at a time.

To keep us from staring up into the clouds—to get us
moving in our work—Jesus uses words like *ask*, *seek*, and
knock (Matthew 7:7). These active words build motion into

our faith. And we live by faith, trusting and following our Lord even when we might wish for more sight.

For faith to be present, action is required.
JANE JARRELL

❖ FOR FURTHER THOUGHT:

Jesus sent the disciples on a mission to change the world. . .with minimal instructions. Why do you think God often gives limited information about what to do next?

❖ PRACTICAL APPLICATION:

When God calls you to do something, how can you be prepared to jump in immediately?

---

*God, I don't know what tomorrow will bring—
but I know You do, and that's all that matters.
Show me how to live moment by moment in faith.*

GOD IS YOUR STRENGTH

Iniquities prevail against me; as for our
transgressions, You shall purify them away.
PSALM 65:3

How often do you mistake being strong in the Lord with simply being strong on your own?

There are no caveats in this psalm about being stronger than your sins. There are no special exceptions for people who are especially determined to conquer their weaknesses and imperfections. Sin *will* sometimes overpower you, no matter how much you may want to choose obedience. This is not to excuse sinning. The Bible says, after all, that one of the fruits of the Spirit is self-control (Galatians 5:22–23). So God does call every Christian man to resist sin.

But you can't make yourself more determined or focused on your own. Thankfully, God has a better way: utter reliance on His mercy and grace. If you want to find your strength each day, you must find God—and that starts with confessing your failures and weaknesses.

Whether you feel overwhelmed and powerless or you're gritting your teeth in determination, you'll never advance to a point that you'll be able to blot out your own sins. If you rely on your strength and willpower, you'll most assuredly lose. But God's mercy will be there to meet you and deliver you. So cry out to Him for His strength.

Once you rest in God, your strength will be endless.

The greatest glory we can give to God is to distrust our own strength utterly, and to commit ourselves wholly to His safe keeping.
BROTHER LAWRENCE

❯ FOR FURTHER THOUGHT:

Do you sometimes feel frustrated because you can't seem to overcome a specific sin?

❯ PRACTICAL APPLICATION:

Identify the sin you struggle with the most, formally relinquish that battle to God today, and then quit trusting in your own power to overcome it. Let God work.

Lord, I'm sick of trying to fight my sin nature on my own. It's a losing battle. That's why I'm surrendering the situation to You— You're the only one who can make me holy.

CALLED TO APPRECIATE

From the rising of the sun to the setting of the same, the Lord's name is to be praised.

PSALM 113:3

Sometimes, you become the good you appreciate in someone else.

This is especially true in praising God. When you appreciate His goodness—when it invades your mind and exits your body in praise—something supernatural happens. The more time you spend praising God deep within your soul, the more attached to Him you become.

When Jehoshaphat faced the terror of approaching armies, he "appointed singers to the Lord and those who should praise the beauty of holiness as they went out before the army" (2 Chronicles 20:21). When they reached the battlefield, their enemies were already dead. So "they returned, every man of Judah and Jerusalem and Jehoshaphat in front of them, to go back to Jerusalem with joy. . . . And they came to Jerusalem, to the house of the Lord, with lyres and harps and trumpets" (verses 27–28).

Unlike his heir who never praised God and who "departed without being desired" (21:20), Jehoshaphat appreciated God and was praised. Similarly, Paul praised God from prison. . .and ended up sharing Jesus with the Roman emperor (Acts 25:12–27).

Appreciating God changes you so much that others eventually can't help but notice.

You can't expect to develop a close friendship with someone whom you totally ignore. You need to acknowledge God's presence, recognize His activity in your lives, and appreciate His provisions.
BRUCE BICKEL AND STAN JANTZ

❯❯ FOR FURTHER THOUGHT:

What are some ways in which you can express this appreciation to others?

❯❯ PRACTICAL APPLICATION:

Practice appreciating God today. Dwell on His nature, consider the ways in which He's blessed you, and meditate on Jesus' sacrifice.

God, I never want to take Your love and blessings for granted. Continually remind me of Your goodness and show me how to conform my mind to the pattern of Your holiness.

A COMMITMENT TO PRAISE GOD

Lord, I have called daily on You; I have
stretched out my hands to You.

Psalm 88:9

If you're honest, you have to admit that Psalm 88 is a gloomy piece of writing. In it, the psalmist first praises God for saving him and then presents a series of sorrowful laments. That's where today's verse comes in—a moment of hope in the midst of his complaints.

Today's psalm is not an easy read, but it challenges us to praise and thank God in easy and difficult times alike. True, this isn't easy when we're going through hardships. But when we praise Him and reach up to Him, even when we don't feel like it, He'll strengthen and encourage us. He may even teach us some wisdom in the midst of our trials.

What does your walk with God look like when your life is difficult, when it seems like God's disappeared in the midst of your troubles? Do you find yourself withdrawing and trying to handle your problems on your own? Or do you spread out your hands to Him, praise His name, and ask Him to bless you through everything?

Sometimes praise is repetitively desperate,
but it is often in these repetitious cries
that purer praise is found.
DAVID CROWDER

❯❯ FOR FURTHER THOUGHT:

How does praising God in the mist of trials lighten
your own spirit as well?

❯❯ PRACTICAL APPLICATION:

The next time something is taken from you, use the
opportunity to thank God for something equally
(or more) important that you still possess.

Heavenly Father, I praise You for Your
greatness and Your love toward me. Even
if everything I have is taken away, I'll
still praise You for preserving my soul.

WORK OUT YOUR OWN SALVATION

But the path of the just is like the shining light
that shines more and more until the perfect
day. The way of the wicked is like darkness;
they do not know what they stumble over.

PROVERBS 4:18–19

Solomon offered a stark contrast in today's verses. The path of the wicked is fraught with danger. Those who take it stumble but aren't even sure what tripped them up. The person who walks the path of the just, however, leaves darkness behind. The farther he goes down the right path, the brighter his path becomes since God's grace completely illuminates it.

The apostle Paul offered a similar message: "Therefore, my beloved, as you have always obeyed, not as in my presence only, but now much more in my absence, work out your own salvation with fear and trembling" (Philippians 2:12). God calls us to trust Him, but He also calls us to work.

What does working out your own salvation look like in your life? What specifically are you doing to flee the way of the wicked in favor of the path of the just? Are you taking responsibility for feeding yourself spiritually? Are you gathering with other believers? Are you staying steadfast in prayer?

In the original language of the New Testament, the word righteousness *literally means "to stay within the lines." These days, no one is really sure where the lines are or who was supposed to draw them. But in a world with no lines, how can we make right choices?*
JOHN TRENT

❯ FOR FURTHER THOUGHT:

Do you sometimes dismiss God's laws for the sake of convenience? Or are you careful to follow His rules, no matter how laborious they may seem?

❯ PRACTICAL APPLICATION:

What guardrails can you put up to obey God more strictly before poor choices land you on a wrong path?

God, guide my footsteps down the path of righteousness. Reveal to me the wicked path so that I can shun it with every effort I have.

BEING A "ONE ANOTHER" BELIEVER

*And let us consider one another to provoke
to love and to good works, not forsaking the
assembling of ourselves together, as is the manner
of some, but exhorting one another, and so much
the more as you see the Day approaching.*

HEBREWS 10:24–25

Have you ever wondered why regularly attending services at a good Bible-teaching church is so important? If not, try looking up the term "one another" in the New Testament and see what it says.

Here are a few examples.

"Be kindly affectionate to one another with brotherly love" (Romans 12:10).

"Receive one another" (Romans 15:7).

"By love serve one another" (Galatians 5:13).

Clearly, this idea of "one another" is important to God. In Paul's time as well as our own, God has called us to reject solitude and join other believers in worshipping Him.

Yes, you can worship God by yourself. You can hear His voice in your personal times of prayer and Bible reading. Nothing, however, can take the place of meeting with other believers in a good church.

Blest be the tie that binds
Our hearts in Christian love;
The fellowship of kindred minds
Is like to that above.
JOHN FAWCETT

›› FOR FURTHER THOUGHT:

What are some ways in which you can bond more deeply with your church friends on other days of the week?

›› PRACTICAL APPLICATION:

If you haven't already, try getting involved with your local church—a men's Bible study, a volunteer program, etc.

Lord, I thank You for the opportunity I have
to meet fellow Christians each week. Show me
how to develop strong friendships with them
as we move forward in our Christian walk.

NEVER STOP LEARNING

*A wise man will hear and will increase learning, and
a man of understanding shall attain wise counsels.*

PROVERBS 1:5

"It is not that I'm so smart," Albert Einstein is quoted as saying, "but I stay with the questions much longer."

Some of us are simply not willing to live with questions. In a world where the answer to every trivial inquiry is right at our fingertips, finding the time (or the desire) to go deeper has become a lost art.

Yet "deeper" is exactly where God calls us to go. Packed schedules and a constant flood of activities have given the concept of quiet contemplation a bad name. For many men, *rest* has turned into a four-letter word. But rest is not laziness. When it comes to finding strength for life's challenges, true rest—a desire to linger over the Word of God—is the only path forward.

Answers to the questions that lurk in the deepest, darkest places in our hearts—the questions we dare not share with anyone—are all found in God's Word. But we must make up our minds to stop passing the buck to others and begin feeding ourselves. A lack of knowledge and real connection with Jesus Christ is nobody's fault but our own.

Nobody's ever truly "heard it all," especially when it comes to God's Word.

Bibles laid open, millions of surprises.
GEORGE HERBERT

>> FOR FURTHER THOUGHT:

Why do you think God wants us to look for answers in
His Word instead of waiting for Him to give them to
us all at once?

>> PRACTICAL APPLICATION:

Rank the two or three most pressing issues you face.
Then sit down with your Bible and diligently search for
solutions.

---

*Lord God, I know all the important answers
in life are found in Your Word. Help me
never to search anywhere else for answers.*

IT'S WORTH TRUSTING GOD

*"What wickedness have your fathers found in
Me, that they have gone far from Me?"*

Jeremiah 2:5

God described how He'd miraculously brought the Jews'
ancestors out of slavery in Egypt, provided for them in a
barren desert, and performed miracles to bring them into the
promised land. Despite all this, His people turned from Him
to worship useless idols. Hence, His rhetorical question above.

The truth was, the Israelites had found no legitimate
fault with God. "He is the Rock. His work is perfect, for all
His ways are judgment, a God of truth and without iniquity"
(Deuteronomy 32:4).

But many modern people think they have found fault
with God. They say, "He allows innocent children to suffer.
Christianity is outdated, out of touch with modern liberated
worldviews." So they disrespect God and stray in their hearts.
Do you sometimes find yourself doing this?

Trust. God's works are still perfect, even though you can't
yet see the end from the beginning. "You *are* good, and *do*
good (Psalm 119:68, emphasis added). Even the most seemingly senseless tragedies will be recycled into a meaningful
design. If you're struggling to trust God, ask Him to help.
Every good and perfect gift comes from Him (James 1:17).

We must never limit God's ability to turn even the worst, most vile experience in our lives into something productive, beneficial, and positive.
CHARLES STANLEY

❯ FOR FURTHER THOUGHT:

Have you ever found it hard to trust God, even after He worked miraculously in your life? Why?

❯ PRACTICAL APPLICATION:

How can you avoid a pessimistic, faithless mindset? What changes can you make to your own attitudes and thoughts?

Father, I'm sometimes tempted to wallow in my despair, but I know You've called me to so much more. Teach me how to trust You in every situation. I know You'll always come through.

MEDITATE ON GOD

"Be still and know that I am God."
PSALM 46:10

There's a time to earnestly pray for what you need, and there's a time to praise God for providing all your needs. But there's *also* a time to meditate, to simply think deeply on who Go is for an extended period. During those times, focus entirely on Him and keep your mind from wandering. God will reward you with a deeper knowledge of His nature and His love.

Some Christians shy away from meditation, thinking that Eastern religions have a monopoly on it. But the Bible spoke of meditation thousands of years ago, long before any modern fads. God commanded, "Be still and know that I am God" (Psalm 46:10). You are to still your heart and focus on knowing Him—that He is almighty God, exalted above all else, supreme, holy, beautiful, and glorious in every way.

You should also meditate on the wonderful things God has done in your life and the lives of others. Think of His miracles, both great and small. "I meditate on all Your works; I muse on the work of Your hands" (Psalm 143:5).

When you read the Bible, don't hurry through it. Pause at a verse and meditate deeply on its meaning. "O how I love Your law! It is my meditation all day long" (Psalm 119:97). Paul said, "Meditate on these things. Give yourself wholly to them" (1 Timothy 4:15).

God calls you to meditate on Him. What better time to start than now?

We ought not to criticize, explain, or judge the scriptures by our mere reason, but diligently, with prayer, meditate thereon, and seek their meaning.
MARTIN LUTHER

❯❯ FOR FURTHER THOUGHT:

How well do you meditate on God's Word each day?

❯❯ PRACTICAL APPLICATION:

If you haven't already, set aside at least fifteen minutes per day to dwell deeply on just a handful of Bible verses, asking God to speak to you in this time of silence.

I think about a lot of things each day, God, yet it's somehow hard to add Your Word to my schedule. Help me to prioritize meditation and to avoid any distractions while doing so.

LET GOD AVENGE YOU

And the king said, "Is there not still
anyone of the house of Saul, that I may
show the kindness of God to him?"

2 Samuel 9:3

When God's Spirit departed from Saul, Israel's first king hunted his replacement, the young shepherd who had played peaceful harmonies to lull his troubled soul. David lived on the run for years, refusing to fight back against God's anointed, even when presented with ideal opportunities to end Saul's life.

David not only passed up taking revenge, but after Saul died in battle, he sought out his remaining descendants to see if he could do them any good.

In David's day, mercy was seen as weakness. To refuse to return a slight to your honor tainted you in most eyes as unreliable. The whole turning-the-other-cheek thing would have been as ridiculous to them as wearing a clown nose to meet your future in-laws would be today.

David demonstrated that the higher virtue lies in being able to avenge yourself but refusing to do so. It takes faith to refrain—a belief that when God said vengeance belonged to Him (Proverbs 25:21–22; Romans 12:19), He meant it. Not only will He hold you accountable for all you've said and done, He'll do the same for everyone else. Have the faith to let Him.

A revengeful spirit is contrary to our heavenly calling.
Thomas Manton

❯ FOR FURTHER THOUGHT:

Why does humanity so often choose revenge as its first option?

❯ PRACTICAL APPLICATION:

The next time you have an opportunity to get back at someone, practice letting go of your anger. Pray for the strength to refuse retaliation, and actively choose not to strike back.

I'm grateful, Lord, that it's not my job to exact justice on anyone. Help me never to take this grave responsibility into my own hands.

FEAR GOD, NOT MAN

Once again David inquired of the Lord, and the
Lord answered him, "Go down to Keilah, for I
am going to give the Philistines into your hand."
1 Samuel 23:4 niv

After learning that enemy soldiers were looting the threshing floor in Keilah—a city in southern Judah near the border with the Philistines—David had one question for the Lord: "Shall I go and strike these Philistines?" (1 Samuel 23:2).

Even though the Lord said yes, David's men weren't ready for battle. They admitted that they were afraid even living in Judah. Perhaps they feared retaliation from King Saul for aligning themselves with David. Maybe they wondered if some among their number were loyal to Saul. So David inquired of the Lord again and was given the same answer. He and his men went to battle and inflicted heavy losses on the Philistines.

We as Christians are like David's men. We will certainly face opposition for standing with Jesus—from friends, coworkers, and maybe even our families. When the Lord sent out His twelve disciples, He promised them opposition (Matthew 10:23; Luke 21:12; John 15:20). But He also told them this: "Do not fear those who kill the body but are not able to kill the soul. But rather fear Him who is able to destroy both soul and body in hell" (Matthew 10:28).

In other words, God calls you to fear Him, not man. He is stronger, wiser, and more loving than we can even imagine. He'll take care of us.

Fear of God can deliver us from the fear of man.
JOHN WITHERSPOON

✦ FOR FURTHER THOUGHT:

Based on your lifestyle and your interactions with others, which kind of fear drives you the most?

✦ PRACTICAL APPLICATION:

How is the "fear" of God different from the fear of man? How can you cultivate the first fear and starve the second?

Father, Your love erases my fear of rejection and even death. Teach me to reverence You and put Your acceptance ahead of man's opinions.

TRUST GOD'S THOUGHTS

"For My thoughts are not your thoughts,
nor are your ways My ways," says the LORD.
Isaiah 55:8

In Isaiah 55:7, God tells the wicked to "abandon his way, and the unrighteous man his thoughts." In verse 8, He explains, "For My thoughts are not your thoughts, nor are your ways My ways." Does that mean if you're saved and obeying God that your thoughts and ways are much closer to His thoughts and ways? Absolutely.

Still, God sees the end of all matters from their beginning and understands everything completely—things that we find incomprehensible. So it's often a quantum leap to trust God's thoughts since what He says usually flies in the face of human logic.

But you've already learned down through the years that appearances are often incorrect. A quote often attributed to Mark Twain says, "When I was a boy of fourteen, my father was so ignorant I could hardly stand to have the old man around. But when I got to be twenty-one, I was astonished at how much he had learned in seven years."

When you get to heaven, you'll have a good laugh about how you once thought you knew better than God.

Man's part is to trust and God's part is to work.
HANNAH WHITALL SMITH

✦ FOR FURTHER THOUGHT:

What "mysteries" do you have in your mind about God? Do these unanswered questions inspire awe, or do they drive you to doubt?

✦ PRACTICAL APPLICATION:

The next time you doubt God's methods, try making a list of the universe's biggest mysteries. After some time, stop and add your current pressing question to the end. Then remind yourself that God knows everything about each item on your list.

I don't know everything, Lord, nor do I pretend to. Help me never be so high-minded that I think I know better than You.

CAST YOUR CARES ON GOD

*Cast your burden on the LORD, and He shall sustain
you; He shall never allow the righteous to be moved.*

PSALM 55:22

This passage of scripture has been a source of great comfort
to millions of believers, yet some people protest. "When huge
problems come," they say, "you simply calmly hand them
to God and He takes care of everything? I *wish!*" This is a
valid point, so let's look at the verse in context.

Earlier in the psalm, David spoke of threats and conspir-
acies, battles raging against him, and the stinging betrayal
of friends. (This likely happened during the civil war when
Absalom revolted.) David confessed his fear, saying, "My
heart is greatly pained within me, and the terrors of death
have fallen on me. Fearfulness and trembling have come on
me" (verses 4–5).

David was eventually able to cast his cares on God and
experience peace, but it wasn't a quick or easy process. He
also had to plan, strategize, and lead his forces against his
enemies' attacks. And he had to pray desperately day after day,
several times a day. He said, "Evening and morning and at
noon I will pray and cry aloud" (verse 17). David *continually*
cast his cares and fears upon God until he finally received
assurance that God had heard him and would answer.

Yes, you can simply calmly hand small problems over
to God. But when huge problems assail you, you may have
to desperately and repeatedly cast your cares on Him. And
He will answer.

*With all your weakness and helplessness, with
all your frailties and infirmities, with all your
sorrows and cares, He invites you to come to Him.*
JOHN DAWSON

›› FOR FURTHER THOUGHT:

Are you persistent in your requests toward God, or are
your prayers less pressing and more casual?

›› PRACTICAL APPLICATION:

Why do you think some Christians grow cynical about
God's ability to provide for them? How can you avoid
this attitude?

---

*Lord, I know You've called me to lean on You for
every problem I face. Teach me to be persistent in
my petitions, even when nothing seems to change.*

THE SOURCE OF POWER

The everlasting God, the LORD, the Creator of the ends of the earth, does not lose strength, nor is weary. . . . He gives power to the faint, and He increases the strength of those who have no might.
ISAIAH 40:28–29

God has absolutely unlimited power. He created the earth and the entire universe full of billions and trillions of stars, but this astonishing feat didn't tire Him out. Even to this day, He still delights in doing the miraculous.

Human beings, however, have definite limitations. A hard day's work wipes them out. A ten-minute run wearies them. Even a stressful day can leave them mentally exhausted. But after writing today's passage, Isaiah went on to explain, "Those who wait on the LORD shall renew their strength" (verse 31).

God can empower you when your batteries are running low. In fact, even if you suffer from permanent disabilities and limitations, God can infuse you with His strength and help you accomplish things that would be impossible even if you had full health and strength.

Once, the apostle Paul asked God to heal a medical condition. God told him, "My grace is sufficient for you, for My strength is made perfect in weakness" (2 Corinthians 12:9). This totally changed Paul's thinking, and he concluded, "I take pleasure in weaknesses. . . . For when I am weak, then I am strong" (verse 10).

You may not necessarily *feel* strong when you have God's strength working through you. But with His strength available, you can accomplish anything you need to do.

There is no end to the power He wants to exhibit in our lives. . . . God can keep his people on fire for him, can keep them sharp and intense.
JIM CYMBALA AND DEAN MERRILL

» FOR FURTHER THOUGHT:

What's the primary difference between your strength and God's?

» PRACTICAL APPLICATION:

Study the ordinary men in the Bible whom God called to great things. Then internalize this message and ask God what His calling is for you today.

Almighty God, I don't always feel strong—in fact, I often feel powerless. Thank You for reassuring me of Your powerful support.

GOD-HONORING HUMILITY

Humble yourselves therefore under the mighty
hand of God, that He may exalt you in due time.
1 Peter 5:6

It's probably fair to say that pride is at the heart of nearly every sin. Pride causes people to boast about themselves and to tear others down. Pride causes people to believe they can do for themselves what God has promised to do for them—which leads to a lack of prayer. Pride causes conflicts between people, and it keeps us from confessing our sins to one another and to God so that we can be reconciled.

This list could go on and on. It's no small wonder that God has said, "I hate pride" (Proverbs 8:13).

God hates human pride, but He loves humility, which can be defined as the acknowledgement that apart from Him, we are nothing and can do nothing of value. When we are humble, we are in effect confessing that we have nothing to offer God apart from what He's already done.

So build your life on the words of the apostle Peter. Humble yourself before God. Don't seek to be exalted on your own but answer God's call to a patient and humbly obedient life.

Here is a wonder! God is on high;
and yet the higher a man lifts up himself,
the farther he is from God; and the lower a
man humbles himself, the nearer he is to God.
THOMAS BROOKS

✦ FOR FURTHER THOUGHT:

How often do you tell others about the good things
you've done?

✦ PRACTICAL APPLICATION:

The next time you do a good deed—volunteering,
offering someone money, etc.—make a conscious effort
to shift the credit from yourself to God.

Lord, help me to hate pride as much as You
do. May I recognize it—and strive to destroy
it—the moment it appears in my soul.

CALLED TO ACCOUNTABILITY

*Confess your faults to one another and pray for
one another, that you may be healed. The effective
fervent prayer of a righteous man avails much.*

JAMES 5:16

As men, we don't enjoy talking with others about our sin struggles. Maybe it's our independent spirit that keeps us from that kind of honest confession. Maybe it's our fear of making ourselves vulnerable to others. Maybe it's our worry about being looked down on because of our real-life struggles.

As uncomfortable as confessing your sin struggles may make us feel, that's exactly what God calls us to do. Today's verse commands believers to come clean with one another so that they can pray for healing and victory for fellow Christians. And when you confess your sins that way, God adds another blessing: accountability.

Life experience says your brothers in Christ likely won't be shocked when you confess a sin you know is holding you back. In fact, when you open this line of communication, you often learn that others struggle with the very same sins. That helps you pray for one another and keep each other accountable. That, in turn, leads to victory for all.

*Choosing to become accountable
to others takes real courage.*
Tom Eisenman

❯❯ FOR FURTHER THOUGHT:

Shame comes in various forms—some healthy and others destructive. How can you tell the difference?

❯❯ PRACTICAL APPLICATION:

Do you have an "accountability partner" in your life? If not, who in your church might be a good candidate to fulfill this vital role?

Lord, I want to be more honest with others about my flaws. Grant me the courage and humility to allow someone else to assist me in my walk with You.

A CLEAN HEART

Create in me a clean heart, O God, and renew a right spirit within me. Do not cast me away from Your presence, and do not take Your Holy Spirit from me. Restore to me the joy of Your salvation.

PSALM 51:10–12

Let's face it: there are some rooms in our "house" we don't want anyone to see. Sure, we intend to clean up our thoughts someday. And we may even do a little work on our habits now and then. But if someone showed up unannounced and asked to have a look around, we would prefer to keep the door to that one certain room tightly closed.

In the Bible, David was an adulterer, a murderer, and a liar. And yet he was known as a man after God's own heart. How could that be? Perhaps the answer resides in the passion with which he always returned to God. After sinning with Bathsheba and killing her husband, Uriah, he cried, "Have mercy on me, O God, according to Your loving-kindness; according to the multitude of Your tender mercies, blot out my transgressions. Wash me thoroughly from my iniquity, and cleanse me from my sin. For I acknowledge my transgressions, and my sin is ever before me. Against You, You only, have I sinned, and done this evil in Your sight" (Psalm 51:1–4).

The devil knows each of us by name, but he calls us out by our sin. Jesus knows our sin, but He calls us by our name. No matter who we are or what we've done, we can always say, "Create in me a clean heart, O God." And He will do it.

*Come boldly into his throne of grace—even
when you have sinned and failed. He forgives—
instantly—those who repent with godly sorrow.*
DAVID WILKERSON

›› FOR FURTHER THOUGHT:

How does God's call for us to repent not only restore
our relationship with Him but ease our own stress and
guilt?

›› PRACTICAL APPLICATION:

How often do you come to God in repentance? Is
there something you should confess right now?

---

*Lord God, I'm far from perfect. In fact, I've made
too many mistakes to count. That's why I'm so
thankful for Your mercy—no matter how low I
sink, You are always there, ready to lift me up.*

ASK FOR THE IMPOSSIBLE

*When they had crossed over. . .Elijah said to
Elisha, "Ask me what I should do for you before I
am taken away from you." And Elisha said, "I ask,
let a double portion of your spirit be upon me."*
2 KINGS 2:9

What a bold request.

Elijah—a leader, prophet, and miracle worker—offered to give a blessing to Elisha. Elisha responded, "Let me inherit a double portion of your spirit." Why would Elisha want the heavy responsibilities and difficulties involved in this type of work?

Elisha could have asked for wealth, unlimited power, or a life with no problems. Even the ability to live each day in peace was within his reach. Yet he asked for Elijah's spirit. He did not ask to have a larger ministry than Elijah—he was only asking to inherit what Elijah was leaving and to be able to carry it on.

Today, God calls each Christian man to ask boldly for the impossible. He deeply desires to bless us. And if our hearts line up with His will and we stay open to His call, He'll take the ordinary and, through His power, transform our prayers into the extraordinary.

It is better to aim at the impossible
than to be content with the inferior.
MABEL HALE

✦ FOR FURTHER THOUGHT:

When was the last time God presented you with an
"impossible" mission?

✦ PRACTICAL APPLICATION:

Ask God to pull you out of your comfort zone and give
you the courage and ability to answer His "impossible"
calling.

Lord, I'm not content to just coast by in life.
Please challenge my faith with big ambitions
and show me how powerful You are.

THE BIGGER PICTURE

Or do you despise the riches of His goodness and patience and long-suffering, not knowing that the goodness of God leads you to repentance?

ROMANS 2:4

Why is patience a virtue? Sometimes, people just need to be corrected—like your kids when they're headed for the wall socket with a fork, that guy at work when he keeps taking your lunch out of the fridge, and your committee at church that's about to make a bad decision about buying a piano.

In those situations, quick action and uncompromising conversations are needed. You're right to act; safety, courtesy, professionalism, and stewardship are at stake. But *how* will you do it? There's the rub.

Think of all the times Jesus' disciples messed up—Peter with his ongoing foot-in-mouth disease or John and James disputing who should be top dog and wanting to call down fire on entire villages. Sometimes, bluntly sharing your mind succeeds only in offending people.

Patience seems to be made up of other virtues—love, mercy, and humility among them. That's why when Jesus corrected His followers' failures, He was gentle, courteous, and polite. He saw a bigger picture—their overarching needs rather than their momentary misdeeds—and He called His followers to do the same.

Consider God's patience when others test yours.

Patience is the virtue that transforms an angry tongue. Patience takes time to hesitate and evaluate. It rejects anger sins. True patience finds its strength in an unflinching focus on God and an unconditional love toward those who have hurt us.
JOSEPH STOWELL

❯❯ FOR FURTHER THOUGHT:

When someone cuts you off in traffic or takes too long at the drive-thru, what is your immediate reaction?

❯❯ PRACTICAL APPLICATION:

How can you take steps to ensure that people always see God's love shining through you—even when they're behaving in unlovable ways?

Father, I know that the people who upset me are often struggling with issues of their own. Help me to be considerate and patient toward them, just as You are toward me.

WORTHY OF THE PROMOTION

*For promotion comes neither from the east nor
from the west nor from the south. But God is the
Judge; He puts down one and sets up another.*

PSALM 75:6–7

In most workplaces, men try their best, hoping to get a promotion to a higher paying, more prestigious job. Everyone has heard the story of a guy who started out in the mailroom and worked his way through the ranks to become the departmental vice president.

Good for that guy!

But today's scripture strongly suggests that in God's kingdom work, *He* puts people on the pathway to promotion. Your part is to do what He has for you to do. . .and to do it well.

Jesus once told the story of a servant who had served his master particularly well. When the master learned of the servant's work, he told him: "Well done, good and faithful servant. You have been faithful over a few things; I will make you ruler over many things. Enter into the joy of your lord" (Matthew 25:21).

God chooses whom He wants to promote. When you show yourself faithful in doing what He has given you to do, you prove yourself worthy of additional assignments.

Spiritual maturity has to do with wanting to do the Father's will for us—not only out of duty but out of overwhelming adoration and devotion. God measures maturity by the level of devotion we display.

JOSEPH STOWELL

⇥ FOR FURTHER THOUGHT:

Why would our attitudes about our tasks matter as much, if not more, than the tasks themselves?

⇥ PRACTICAL APPLICATION:

When God gives you an assignment—say, volunteering in your local church—resist the urge to give it only minimal effort. Rather, ask Him to give you an enthusiasm and zeal that shines through in your hard work.

You've given me a lot of responsibility, God, and I don't want to fail You. Give me the grace and wisdom to fulfill my calling exactly the way You want.

CALLED TO GRATITUDE

Give thanks in everything, for this is the will
of God in Christ Jesus concerning you.
1 THESSALONIANS 5:18

Yes, Paul actually is saying to thank God no matter *what* circumstance you find yourself in. Even when you're having a terrible day, you are to have a grateful attitude and to give audible thanks. It's God's calling for you.

Can you trust Him on this one? Does God really expect this of you? Yes. Jesus tells you to count yourself blessed when persecuted. He said, "Rejoice in that day and leap for joy, for, behold, your reward is great in heaven" (Luke 6:23). After being beaten for Jesus' sake, the apostles "departed. . .rejoicing that they were counted worthy to suffer shame for His name" (Acts 5:41). And Paul and Silas sang praises to God after being beaten (Acts 16:22–25).

This may be shaping up to be one of your least favorite commandments, but give it a chance. God advises it for your own good. If you're consistently thankful, even in serious troubles, you'll (a) have a much happier life overall; (b) make it through rough times more easily; and (c) be greatly rewarded in heaven.

*When your mouth is filled with gratitude
and thanksgiving, there simply won't
be room for false or cynical words.*
RON MEHL

❯❯ FOR FURTHER THOUGHT:

Why would Jesus tell His followers to rejoice when they are persecuted for Him?

❯❯ PRACTICAL APPLICATION:

Purposefully decide to praise God in the midst of a hardship and observe how the choice affects your overall disposition.

---

*Lord Jesus, it's hard to have joy sometimes,
especially when life's deck seems stacked against me.
During these times, remind me of Your goodness
and of my reward that awaits at the end.*

STRONGER THAN SAMSON

*And he was very thirsty and called on the L*ORD
*and said, "You have given this great deliverance
into the hand of your servant, and now shall
I die of thirst and fall into the hand of the
uncircumcised?" But God split a hollow place that
is in Lehi, and water came out of it. And when
he drank, his spirit came again and he revived.*

JUDGES 15:18–19

After taking out a mass of Philistine soldiers with a makeshift weapon, Samson sang a brief song: "With the jawbone of a donkey, heaps on heaps, with the jaw of a donkey I have slain a thousand men" (Judges 15:16). Then he realized he was thirsty, which may have been an aspect of God's discipline on the willful judge of Israel.

Samson's thirst was "a natural effect of the great pains he had taken," John Wesley wrote. "And perhaps there was the hand of God therein, to chastise him for not making mention of God in his song, and to keep him from being proud of his strength."

Even Samson's prayer above has an edge to it. He seemed exasperated by his thirst and God's "abandonment" of him. But in His mercy, God miraculously provided water.

That's the amazing thing about God: He often blesses us with good things even when we fail Him—when our hearts are cold and distracted by willful sin—and then calls us to acknowledge His blessings.

Today, let's root out any attitudes and actions that might separate us from God. If we can consistently do that, we'll be stronger than Samson ever was.

The prayer of a Christian is not an attempt to force God's hand, but a humble acknowledgment of helplessness and dependence.
J. I. PACKER

❯ FOR FURTHER THOUGHT:

When has God given you a second chance after you made a mess of things?

❯ PRACTICAL APPLICATION:

How can we prevent God's mercies from slipping out of our memories?

Lord, thank You for stepping in and undoing the spiritual catastrophes I've caused in my life. Help me to never take Your unending grace for granted.

TRAINING IN GODLY LIVING

Uzziah was sixteen years old when he began to reign,
and he reigned fifty-two years in Jerusalem. . . . And
he sought God in the days of Zechariah, who had
understanding through the visions of God, and as
long as he sought the LORD, God made him prosper.
2 CHRONICLES 26:3, 5

God calls you to endure for the sake of His name and *with His help*. He sends people to help when you think you walk alone. Some resist or even refuse the help, but God knows two are better than one.

Uzziah became Judah's king at the age of sixteen. Maybe you can't imagine a teen becoming a nation's ruler, but this young man ruled as a good king for more than half a century. How? Because he didn't work alone. Zechariah, a preacher by trade, came to the rescue by mentoring the king. This friendship resulted in a godly leadership. Uzziah had help.

If you're following God but trying to do it alone, you would do well to begin following Uzziah's example. Find someone who has pursued God longer than you have, and learn, grow, and serve together. Get some training in godly living, and you'll find it much easier to endure the next hard day.

*The value of mentoring derives
from the value of relationships.*
HOWARD AND WILLIAM HENDRICKS

❯ FOR FURTHER THOUGHT:

How close of a friendship do you have with an older man (or men) at church?

❯ PRACTICAL APPLICATION:

Get to know one of these older men even better. Ask him for advice whenever possible and listen as he describes his past successes and failures.

---

*Father, thank You for sending godly older people
into my life. Help me to be attentive enough to
recognize their wisdom and seek their help.*

PEACE AND STRENGTH THROUGH GOD'S WORD

Those who love Your law have great peace,
and nothing shall offend them.

PSALM 119:165

The writer of the epistle to the Hebrews once wrote of scripture, "For the word of God is living and powerful and sharper than any two-edged sword, piercing even to the dividing of soul and spirit, and of the joints and marrow, and is a discerner of the thoughts and intentions of the heart" (Hebrews 4:12).

That's a great summary of the role the Bible plays in the life of the believer. And there are even more great benefits of spending time reading and studying the Word: it brings us peace and strength for our walk.

The writer of Psalm 119 points out that the words in the Bible (he refers to it as God's "law") have an amazing ability not just to bring us that inner peace God wants us to live in but to keep us from stumbling into sin.

Have you been lacking peace lately? Does it seem like your life in Christ lacks power? Do you find that you're not walking with Jesus as much as you are stumbling through life? It may be a matter putting your time spent reading and studying the Bible higher—maybe *much* higher—on your list of priorities.

Life in the twenty-first century is busy. Work, family,

home projects, and friends all vie for our time. But if we want the peace and strength that we need to live the life God calls us to, we can't afford to miss out on time with Him and His Word.

I challenge you—dig deep in God's Word and find the nugget of God's glory on every page.
TIM WALTER

❯ FOR FURTHER THOUGHT:

Why is it often difficult to find time for God's Word?

❯ PRACTICAL APPLICATION:

How might you ensure that Bible study doesn't get overshadowed by other daily events?

I want to get to know You better, God, and the only way I can do so is by studying Your Word. Grant me the willpower to consciously set aside time each day to dwell on its truths.

KIND WORDS

Pleasant words are like a honeycomb,
sweet to the soul and health to the bones.
PROVERBS 16:24

You've probably heard it said that you catch more flies with honey than vinegar. Humans tend to respond better to kindness and affirming words than to criticism and browbeating.

People in all kinds of professional endeavors—from high-power business leaders to workaday construction foremen—have figured out their employees tend to perform better when given verbal pats on the back for their good work.

Think the same thing might work with your wife, children, friends, or coworkers? Well, if you take the wisdom of today's verse to its logical conclusion. . .yes, it would!

So if you want to see the best in the people God has put in your life (and who doesn't?), make it a point to speak words of kindness to them. Go out of your way to let them know you notice their efforts. Make it a point to tell them you appreciate them for the things they do and for who they are.

The results might pleasantly surprise you.

*Next to spiritual commitment and physical
survival, the greatest need of a human being is
to be understood, affirmed, and appreciated.*
J. ALLAN PETERSEN

❖ FOR FURTHER THOUGHT:

Which do you prefer most—being criticized or being
supported, even if that support involves a correction?

❖ PRACTICAL APPLICATION:

If you need to correct somebody's mistake—whether
it's a coworker or one of your kids—find a way to end
your correction with a compliment.

---

*Lord, it's so easy to thoughtlessly accept help
from others. But You've called me to a greater
life—one that's filled with kindness and love.
Help me model this love to others today.*

CALLED TO HOSPITALITY

*...distributing to the needs of the
saints, given to hospitality.*
Romans 12:13

The ancient Hebrews were urged to show kindness and hospitality to strangers by taking them into their homes for the night (Job 31:32). And they were expected to feed and protect any guests under their roof. Examples of this include Lot taking in two strangers (who turned out to be angels) in Sodom and the old man in Gibeah taking in the man from Ephraim and his concubine (Genesis 19:1–3; Judges 19:14–21).

These days, such hospitality is rare. With crime and exploitation running rampant, it's considered dangerous and unadvisable. (Granted, we *should* use wisdom when inviting strangers into our homes for the night!)

But God still calls us to be "*given* to hospitality" (Romans 12:13, emphasis added). So let's look at other important ways of showing hospitality. What if a new family comes to your church, doesn't know anyone, and needs friends? Are you eager to reach out to them? Do you talk with your wife about inviting them over for lunch? Do you help them get settled into your town?

Or what if a poor family in your church is struggling, in need of warm clothes, food, or other necessities? Do you simply smile, wave, and say, "Depart in peace; be warmed and filled" (James 2:16), or do you reach out in practical ways to help them?

Keep your eyes open. There are many ways to be "a lover of hospitality" today (Titus 1:8).

Hospitality is the social staff of life, a starting point for discourse and interaction.
THEA JARVIS

» FOR FURTHER THOUGHT:

What did Jesus say about who you're really helping when you help others (Matthew 25:31–46)?

» PRACTICAL APPLICATION:

Do you know of anyone in your church or community who could use a good meal or even a place to stay tonight? If so, how willing are you to take action?

Lord God, I know You want me to show hospitality to others, but I'm often hesitant for safety or even convenience purposes. Help me overcome these barriers and start reaching out today.

THE LEGACY THAT LASTS

Therefore Levi has no part or inheritance with
*his brothers; the L*ORD *is his inheritance.*

DEUTERONOMY 10:9

Are you going to inherit a classic car, a painting by Caravaggio, a vintage book, some land, or money?

Maybe you've inherited some things already.

Everyone understands the happiness an inheritance can bring. It can provide you with things to celebrate and talk about. So. . .what kind of inheritance are you *leaving*?

The Levites were an Old Testament family who refused to worship a golden calf their relatives had made while Moses was receiving the Ten Commandments. Because of their love for God, the Lord gave the Levites more than their relatives' inheritance—He made Himself their inheritance.

You could leave a car or a painting, or you could leave those things and something more. Moses wrote down God's words: "Therefore you shall lay up these words of Mine in your heart and in your soul. . . . And you shall teach them to your children, speaking of them when you sit in your house and when you walk by the way, when you lie down and when you rise up" (Deuteronomy 11:18–19).

Living "these words" in the ordinary moments of every day will help you leave the kind of legacy that lasts.

*The true legacy of a servant will not be
determined by what he has done but by what
others do as a result of what he has done.*
WAYNE CORDEIRO

» FOR FURTHER THOUGHT:

Honestly speaking, how do you think people see you—
as kindhearted and generous or in a less positive light?

» PRACTICAL APPLICATION:

How can you lay the groundworks for a good legacy?
What are you doing right now?

---

*Father, I know I can't take anything with me
when I die. . .but I want the things I leave
behind to truly matter. Show me how to build
a godly legacy for the next generation.*

GODLY PAYBACK

Not rendering evil for evil or reviling for reviling,
but on the contrary, blessing, knowing that you are
called to this, that you should inherit a blessing.
1 Peter 3:9

How do you respond when someone— carelessly or intentionally—does you wrong? It's a rare man who doesn't respond with anger and a thirst for revenge. But while anger may sometimes be justified, God says that your response to someone who does you wrong is to *bless* that person.

Our fallen human nature balks at this command. *I'm entitled to a little vengeance,* we think as our minds compose a sharp, brilliantly crafted comeback. But God tells us that our response to evil should be compassionate, kind, and understanding.

On a purely practical level, you must remember that you can't know what's going on inside the mind of a person who offended you. But God does, and that's one of the reasons He tells you to repay evil with blessings.

No one likes being hurt or insulted. But as a Christian, you must see those unpleasant moments not as negatives but as opportunities to bless those who need God's touch in their lives—and to receive God's blessings on yourself.

Retribution has no place in the life of any Christian.
Jo Berry

❯❯ FOR FURTHER THOUGHT:

When have you tried to take revenge? Did it make you feel better or solve anything at all?

❯❯ PRACTICAL APPLICATION:

The next time you're tempted to pass up mercy in favor of revenge, think of what would happen if God did the same to you.

Father, thank You for not taking revenge on me for the many times I've dishonored Your name. Please grant me the same degree of mercy in my dealings with other people.

SHOWING KINDNESS

And the men of Judah came, and there they anointed David king over the house of Judah. And they told David, saying, "The men of Jabesh-gilead were those who buried Saul." And David sent messengers to the men of Jabesh-gilead and said to them, "You are blessed of the LORD that you have shown this kindness to your lord, to Saul, and have buried him."

2 SAMUEL 2:4–5

After David was anointed king of Israel in Hebron, he learned that the men of Jabesh-gilead had buried the former king, Saul, who had fallen in battle. Very likely, David inquired about Saul's body because he wanted to honor him with a proper burial. Some people, knowing the animosity Saul had shown toward David, might have thought the new king would disapprove of the burial. But David sent a blessing on the men of Jabesh-gilead.

Regardless of how far Saul ended up going astray, he was the Lord's anointed, and worthy of respect. David always had a firm understanding of this concept, even when he was running from Saul, fearing for his life. This is consistent with the Bible's commands to respect authority and treat our enemies with kindness.

Proverbs 24:17–18 says, "Do not rejoice when your enemy falls, and do not let your heart be glad when he stumbles, lest the LORD see it, and it displease Him, and

He turn away His wrath from him."

How do you respond when one of your enemies falls—either literally or figuratively? How does that compare with today's verse?

We think that we do well to be angry with the rebellious, and so we prove ourselves to be more like Jonah than Jesus.
CHARLES SPURGEON

❯❯ FOR FURTHER THOUGHT:

Why do you think God warns against rejoicing at the judgment He deals out on others?

❯❯ PRACTICAL APPLICATION:

How can you start praying positively for an enemy today instead of hoping for his fall?

Father God, I'm sometimes tempted to rejoice when an enemy "gets what he deserves." Remind me that I too deserve judgment—then teach me how to show compassion to others.

WHEN WINTER ENDS

For, behold, the winter is past. The rain is over
and gone. The flowers appear on the earth. The
time of the singing of birds has come, and the
voice of the turtledove is heard in our land.

SONG OF SOLOMON 2:11–12

In ancient times, just like today, winter was a hard time, a season to be endured. Of course, winter in Israel was not usually accompanied by the subzero temperatures and heavy snows common to much of North America.

Still, spring was a time of rejoicing. The cold winter rains had passed, and signs of life were reappearing. Flowers began to bud. Birds began mating. The low, contented cooing of doves could be heard. It was a happy time, "the time of the singing of birds."

Like it or not, all of us go through winter seasons—times of prolonged sorrow when we're nearly overwhelmed by feelings of hopelessness and despair. But God's promise remains true: "Weeping may endure for a night, but joy comes in the morning" (Psalm 30:5).

Even in the harshest of winters, God calls us to anticipate spring. Never give up hope!

*The spring would not be so pleasant as it
is if it did not succeed the winter.*
MATTHEW HENRY

❖ FOR FURTHER THOUGHT:

Why doesn't God always step in and stop our suffering
as soon as we ask?

❖ PRACTICAL SUGGESTION:

Use the next trial—whether it's a financial issue, marital problem, or sickness—as an opportunity to steel
your faith in God. Then, when He finally steps
in, show Him the gratitude He deserves.

---

*Thank You, God, for promising peace in the midst of
life's most unpeaceful moments. Help me remember
that Your goodness remains—even when I can't see it.*

STRENGTH AGAINST LUST

"You have heard that it was said by those of old,
'You shall not commit adultery.' But I say to you
that whoever looks on a woman to lust after her has
already committed adultery with her in his heart."

Matthew 5:27–28

Defense attorneys look for legal loopholes to help their clients avoid punishment. That's a defense attorney's job—and it is something we all tend to do for ourselves. Jesus knew this, and that's why He addressed "loopholes" in His famous sermon on the mount.

While the act of adultery is clearly prohibited in Exodus 20:14, Jesus wanted His hearers to understand the spirit of the law. While some might question whether premarital sex or pornography should be considered adultery, Jesus went to the root of the issue by prohibiting lust.

God created sexual desire as a good thing within marriage. Lust, however, is something else. Pastor John Piper defines it as "taking a perfectly good thing that God created—namely, sexual desire—and abstracting it or stripping it off from an honor toward a person and stripping it off from a supreme regard for God's holiness. You take God away, and you take the honor of man away, and what you have left in sexual desire is lust."

If you struggle with lust, God calls you to stop looking for loopholes to justify sinful activity. The heart of the issue is not what your eyes see but who has your attention. Admit your weakness to God, and then keep your eyes on Him and His holiness. Commit your desires—even your sexual desires—to God's purposes and trust Him to take care of you.

Your flesh, creative and cool as it is, will invariably remind you of a dozen ways to rationalize around the wrong of your lust. And there is a name for those who listen to those reasons: victim.
CHARLES SWINDOLL

⟩ FOR FURTHER THOUGHT:

How often do you struggle with lust? What do you think might be the root cause?

⟩ PRACTICAL APPLICATION:

What perspective on God might make it easier for you to resist lust?

Holy God, teach me to honor You with my eyes and thoughts—not just with my actions. Give me a pure mind that can expel the filth that tries to enter.

GENEROSITY

But I say this: he who sows sparingly
shall also reap sparingly, and he who sows
bountifully shall also reap bountifully.
2 CORINTHIANS 9:6

Generosity is long remembered. So is stingy selfishness!

Scrooge, the main character in Dickens' *A Christmas Carol*, has become the epitome of stingy selfishness—of a man so concerned with himself that he ignored the needs of everyone around him, including his family, employees, and neighbors. But after his dramatic encounter with the ghosts of Christmas past, present, and future, he becomes so generous that "it was always said of him, that he knew how to keep Christmas well, if any man alive possessed the knowledge."

Like Scrooge, we would do well to consider generosity in light of our past, present, and future. God is generous with His children in giving us far more than we need and treating us far better than we deserve. His generosity is best expressed in His most generous gift—His own Son, Jesus. It's impossible to imagine a more generous gift to any less deserving.

Today's verse reminds us that both stingy selfishness and joyous generosity have future consequences. A large measure of our future joy, in this world and the next, depends on generosity today. True generosity isn't about how much; it's possible to give a great deal and not be truly generous.

Rather, it's a matter of a heart that's attuned to a generous God. It's the result of gratitude for what He has done for us and will continue to do.

At the core of the generous person's heart is this penchant for Christ's love—the desire to receive it and to give it to everyone along the way who is in need.
GORDON MACDONALD

❯ FOR FURTHER THOUGHT:

How might a greater understanding of what God has done for you increase your generosity toward others?

❯ PRACTICAL APPLICATION:

When was the last time someone was generous toward you? How did it make you feel? How can you give that same feeling to someone else today?

Lord, it's easy to be stingy and self-indulgent, but I know You've called me to so much more. Help me live up to this calling today by helping someone in need.

A SECOND LOOK

"You shall love your neighbor as yourself."
LEVITICUS 19:18

Many Christians have never actually read the book of Leviticus. As far as they can see from skimming its pages, it contains endless lists of tedious and outdated laws, regulations, and instructions on how to sacrifice animals and stay ritually pure. The book of Deuteronomy, they feel, is almost as irrelevant.

Yet the two greatest commandments in the Bible are found in these books.

When a Pharisee asked Jesus, "Which is the great commandment in the law?" Jesus didn't quote any of the well-known Ten Commandments. Instead, He quoted Deuteronomy 6:5: "You shall love the LORD your God with all your heart." Jesus then stated emphatically, "This is the first and great commandment. And the second is like it." He then quoted Leviticus 19:18: "You shall love your neighbor as yourself" (Matthew 22:34–40).

If the two most important commands in the law are found in these "dull" books, what else might be found there that can inspire and guide us? God calls you to stray off the beaten path of your scripture reading sometimes and explore the remote corners of your Bible. Many wonderful gems are hidden there.

Our Bibles aren't meant to sit on our shelves in pristine condition but are meant to be worn down with daily use.
MICHAEL YOUSSEF

❯❯ FOR FURTHER THOUGHT:

What parts of your Bible do you usually read and study? What parts do you typically avoid?

❯❯ PRACTICAL APPLICATION:

What are some ways you can apply the more obscure passages to your life? Be creative!

Lord, You've given me so many treasures in the form of Your Word. I don't want to just skim its surface—I want to dive deeply into it like an ocean. Open my eyes to these hidden riches today.

AN UNDIVIDED HEART

Teach me Your way, O LORD; I will walk in
Your truth. Unite my heart to fear Your name.
PSALM 86:11

Jesus told His disciples something that resonates with many today: "Do not seek what you shall eat or what you shall drink, nor be of doubtful mind. For the nations of the world seek after all these things, and your Father knows that you have need of these things. But rather seek the kingdom of God, and all these things shall be added to you" (Luke 12:29–31).

Was Jesus saying that you shouldn't concern yourself with providing for yourself and your family? Not at all! The Bible warns that a man who doesn't care for his family is "worse than an unbeliever" (1 Timothy 5:8).

Rather, Jesus' point echoed the words of King David in today's scripture. Yes, a godly man works to care for himself and his family, but he doesn't allow those tasks to distract him from God. Instead, he relies on God's faithfulness so that he can keep his heart from becoming divided.

Worldly necessities can distract you from your relationship with your heavenly Father. So God calls you to set your heart on Him and His eternal kingdom first—and then allow Him to meet your needs here on earth.

The restless, high-pressure hurry in which men live
endangers the very foundations of personal religion.
J. C. RYLE

❯❯ FOR FURTHER THOUGHT:

Satan sometimes uses good things (work, family, and friends) to distract us from the *best* things (God and His kingdom). How can you maintain the proper perspective?

❯❯ PRACTICAL APPLICATION:

How would you rank the relative importance of these people and things in your life? God, your wife, children, the workplace, money, interests and activities, etc.

God, I want to be productive in my work, but
I never want to let productivity interfere with
my relationship with You. Keep my priorities
straight, especially when my schedule is full.

KEEP SMILING

"If I laughed at them, they did not believe it.
And the light of my face they did not cast down."
JOB 29:24

This verse prompts a question: If we communicated solely through our actions or mere presence, without the luxury of words, what message would our lives convey?

It is said that a smile is the light of one's countenance. Job was a righteous, well-respected man of God. His friends and countrymen lauded him for his wisdom, and all men listened to him, heeding his instruction. Prior to Job's afflictions, the people sought his favor. Consequently, his smile was enough to encourage and lighten their loads (verses 21–24).

Our preoccupation with words often obscures a simple truth: *what we say is not as important as who we are.* Job's smile made a difference only because of the life he led.

Our most authentic forms of communication occur without a word. Rather, they flow from an understanding smile, a compassionate touch, a loving gesture, a gentle presence, or an unspoken prayer.

God used Job—an ordinary man whose only adornment was righteous living and a warm smile. And He wants to use us too.

Core convictions are revealed by our
daily actions, by what we actually do.
JOHN ORTBERG

❯❯ FOR FURTHER THOUGHT:

When you say you love someone—your wife, child, or
neighbor—how is that statement proven true?

❯❯ PRACTICAL APPLICATION:

Think of someone in your life who for you is the
embodiment of kindness—then try your best to imi-
tate that person's behavior in each of your interactions.

Kind words take little effort, God—I want to
go far deeper. Teach me to prove my words with
actions instead of merely stopping at the first step.

FIVE THINGS TO HATE

The fear of the LORD is to hate evil; I hate pride and arrogance and the evil way and the perverse mouth.

PROVERBS 8:13

It might surprise you to learn that it's not only kosher to hate certain things—if you love God, it's actually required.

First of all, if you fear God, you are to hate evil. No surprises there. The Bible clearly states, "You who love the LORD, hate evil" (Psalm 97:10). And in case you think hating evil is just an Old Testament concept, note that this command is repeated nearly word for word in the New Testament, where Paul writes, "Hate what is evil" (Romans 12:9). You shouldn't hate people, but you should definitely hate evil whenever you see it.

You are also to hate proud and arrogant attitudes, evil behavior, and evil speech. This can quickly go sour, however, if you start hating these things first and foremost in *others*. This can cause you to have a critical and smug attitude. Even worse, it will create blind spots for these sins in your own life, thus defeating the purpose altogether!

A psalmist prayed, "Search *me*, O God, and know my heart: test *me*, and know *my* thoughts, and see if there is any wicked way in *me*" (Psalm 139:23–24, emphasis added).

God calls us to hate sin, even if—especially if—we find it in ourselves.

*God judges sin because He loathes what it does
to us and to others. He wants us to loathe sin,
too—and be its executioner. If we don't, He will.*
DAVID ROPER

❯ FOR FURTHER THOUGHT:

When it comes to the Christian's words and behavior, what's the diffcrence between hating the sin and hating the sinner?

❯ PRACTICAL APPLICATION:

How well do you think you do in maintaining this important distinction in your own life?

---

*Sin is no laughing matter, God, so I want to
hate it with every fiber of my being. Help me
to never even entertain the idea of sinning,
no matter how tempting it may be.*

CALLED TO REMEMBER

*I remember the days of old; I meditate on
all Your works; I muse on the work of Your
hands. I stretch out my hands to You; my
soul thirsts for You, like a thirsty land.*
PSALM 143:5–6

It's believed that David composed this psalm while on the run after Absalom's rebellion. Surely, he was recalling the days of old when God continually delivered him from Saul's hands. And in remembering God's faithfulness, he entered worship mode, lifting his hands in his thirst for the Lord. In so doing, he provided an example.

Are you going through a familiar trial right now—one you've endured in the past but hoped to never face again? Remember the days of long ago. Remember God's faithfulness.

Consult your journal or talk to the person who prayed with you and walked with you through the trial the first time. Doing so will remind you about the little ways God provided. It will fill you with great hope that God will indeed show up again. Then allow those memories to lead you into a spirit and time of worship.

*Remembering becomes a tool that sees us through
present pain and difficulties and propels us into new,
faith-filled spaces, preparing us for the future.*
LOIS EVANS

❯ FOR FURTHER THOUGHT:

God often uses our memories of past trials to increase
our confidence in Him. How might this fact put your
future trials into perspective?

❯ PRACTICAL APPLICATION:

Write down each time God delivers you from a
worst-case scenario—a financial disaster, injury,
or even death. Then consult this list whenever your
next trial comes.

---

*Lord, I know You want me to remember the times
You've rescued me. Help me to be attentive to Your
intervention each time I face a troubling situation.*

"BE HOLY IN ALL YOU DO"

"You shall be holy to Me, for I the LORD am holy."

LEVITICUS 20:26

Sometimes, a truth or command is so important that the Bible repeats it over and over. That's certainly the case with today's key verse, which is the fifth time the Lord makes this statement in ten chapters of Leviticus (see also 11:44, 11:45, 19:2, and 20:7).

Some may be tempted to think: *But that was then. This is now. Holiness is impossible. Besides, the Lord forgives all my sins.*

Really? Listen to the apostle Peter's emphatic words: "Therefore prepare your mind for action. Be sober, and hope to the end for the grace that is to be brought to you at the revelation of Jesus Christ. As obedient children, not fashioning yourselves according to the former lusts in your ignorance, but as He who has called you is holy, so you be holy in all manner of conduct, because it is written, 'Be holy, for I am holy.' And if you call on the Father, who without partiality judges according to every man's work, pass the time of your sojourning here in fear" (1 Peter 1:13–17).

After love, holiness is the hallmark of the man of God. It doesn't mean that you never sin. But it does mean you keep short accounts with God. It means you forsake old ways of living. It means you focus on heaven. It means you seek God's "well done!"

*God is working in your attitudes and in
your character in ways that will make you
a gracious reflection of His holiness.*
Roy Lessin

» FOR FURTHER THOUGHT:

What's one area of your life—your workplace,
conversations, pastimes, or something else—
that could use more holiness?

» PRACTICAL APPLICATION:

Instead of viewing holiness as a mysterious, nebulous
standard, try breaking it down into smaller segments
and work on them one day at a time.

---

*Lord, I know You've called me to be holy, but I
also know how impossible that task is without
Your help. Reveal to me any unholiness in
my life—and then help me root it out.*

LET GO OF GRUDGES

"Therefore if you bring your gift to the altar, and there remember that your brother has anything against you, leave your gift there before the altar, and go your way. First be reconciled to your brother, and then come and offer your gift."

MATTHEW 5:23–24

Your worship and your treatment of others are linked. Broken fellowship with a neighbor or colleague can get in the way of your worship of God, and the only way to rise above this mess is through confession and forgiveness.

Perhaps your own pride has offended someone, or maybe a grudge has poisoned a relationship. If you give in to anger or demand your rights, you'll cause even more division and alienate yourself from others. The same things that damage your relationships will damage your ability to pray and worship freely.

Pride—whether before God or before others—is always destructive. A grudge could point to a self-righteousness that keeps you from either receiving God's mercy or showing it to others. Anger counteracts the humility that keeps you in your place before God.

If you want to know where you stand before God, look first at your relationships with others. Do your interactions indicate that you think too highly of yourself? What steps can you take to remedy that?

The heaviest thing to carry is a grudge.
L. James Harvey

❯❯ FOR FURTHER THOUGHT:

What methods has God used to help you control your anger?

❯❯ PRACTICAL APPLICATION:

When someone does you wrong, how long does it typically take for your anger to simmer down? How might you improve your record?

Lord, I know it's never a good idea to hold a grudge, yet I sometimes do it anyway. I need Your patience and grace to overcome this tendency so that I can be an effective witness for You.

THE TWO COMMANDMENTS

And Jesus answered him, "The first of all the commandments is 'Hear, O Israel: The Lord our God is one Lord. And you shall love the Lord your God with all your heart and with all your soul and with all your mind and with all your strength.' This is the first commandment. And the second—namely this— is similar: 'You shall love your neighbor as yourself.' There is no other commandment greater than these."

MARK 12:29–31

Jesus was unequivocal about what the Law's most important commandments were. In fact, He stated in Matthew 22:40, "On these two commandments hang all the Law and the Prophets."

Interestingly, neither is found in the Ten Commandments, which usually get more attention and discussion. Does that mean the Ten Commandments aren't important? No, it means the ten are written upon the two concepts Jesus mentioned in the same way they'd been written on two tablets of stone. The Ten Commandments can't be applied or even understood correctly apart from these two commandments.

Now, if you thought the ten were tough to obey, these two are utterly impossible. That's because no commandment of God can be truly obeyed if the heart's not involved. Simple outward adherence is just legalism—it isn't enough. Instead, you desperately need the one who fulfilled God's Law (Matthew 5:17)—particularly the Two Commandments—to live in you and obey it through you. That's the only way.

All true morality, inward and outward,
is comprehended in love, for love is the
foundation of all the commandments.
MEISTER ECKHART

❯ FOR FURTHER THOUGHT:

Why do you think God said that love—for Him and for others—is the foundation for all His commandments?

❯ PRACTICAL APPLICATION:

Based on God's standard of love, how well are you living up to His commandments?

Lord, may I never treat Your commands like mere
duties. Fill me with a passionate, burning love
for righteousness and justice so that I can live
up to the abundant life You've called me to.

DIGNITY FOR THE DOWNCAST

Blessed is he who considers the poor.
The LORD will deliver him in time of trouble.
PSALM 41:1

Being at the bottom looking up is no fun, but it can be the start of a climb. Delving down among the downcast seems hard, but it's an opportunity for a rescue mission.

Resolve to take what you know about endurance and help someone else endure. Don't step on others when they're down—help them up whenever you can. You might be thinking this only applies to places like soup kitchens and homeless shelters, but God also calls you to provide assistance to any friends, neighbors, or family members who might need it.

Helping others is all about showing the same love God has shown you. It's not judgmental. (Though that doesn't mean you ignore sin and its impact.) The greatest help you can offer comes by inviting God to accompany you—letting the words from His book flow from your mouth. Let His grace, love, and mercy shine through in your response to the struggler. As odd as it may sound, you can reduce the intensity of your own struggle by helping others through theirs.

God became earth's mockery to save His children.
How absurd to think that such nobility would
go to such poverty to share such a treasure
with such thankless souls. But He did.
MAX LUCADO

›› FOR FURTHER THOUGHT:

Why does God allow some people to struggle
financially, emotionally, or physically? Why has
He allowed struggles in your own life?

›› PRACTICAL APPLICATION:

Try befriending a poverty-stricken individual whom
you've seen many times but never talked to. This will
help you better understand what that person is going
through.

God, I know You see every person on the planet as a
precious treasure. Give me Your eyes so that I can see
the value in those whom the world counts valueless.

HOW TO TREAT YOUR ENEMIES

And the LORD gave them rest all around, according to all that He swore to their fathers. And not a man of all their enemies stood before them. The LORD delivered all their enemies into their hand.

JOSHUA 21:44

The Bible has a lot to say about enemies. Jesus said, "Love your enemies, bless those who curse you, do good to those who hate you, and pray for those who despitefully use you and persecute you" (Matthew 5:44). But another time, He said, "The LORD said to my Lord, 'Sit on My right hand, until I make Your enemies Your footstool'" (Matthew 22:44, quoting from Psalm 110:1).

The implication is that if you follow Christ and live out His commands, you *will* have enemies in this life. Even so, your job is to love and pray for those opponents while turning the other cheek (see Matthew 5:39). God, however, will ultimately deliver His people's enemies into their hands, turning them into footstools. We never need to plot revenge, no matter how poorly others have treated us. We can simply follow Jesus' higher calling and leave the judgment to God.

And you may find even more than rest. Perhaps the love you show to enemies might break through their hard hearts and usher them into the kingdom.

*Returning evil for evil is the childish attitude
of "he did this to me so I'll do this to him."*
JO BERRY

❯ FOR FURTHER THOUGHT:

When have you held a grudge? How long did it last?
How did it feel holding the grudge, and then letting
it go?

❯ PRACTICAL APPLICATION:

Right now, think of someone you don't like, and pray
for—not against—that person. Continue doing this
each day until any bitter thoughts are gone. Then think
of another person. . .and repeat.

*Lord Jesus, You love everyone, even the people
who nailed You to the cross. Please enable
me to follow Your perfect example.*

CALLED TO ENCOURAGE

Pleasant words are like a honeycomb,
sweet to the soul and health to the bones.
PROVERBS 16:24

Are you an encourager? Does the mood lighten when you enter a room? Do you find yourself talking mostly about yourself, or do you focus on the other person in the conversation?

The tongue is a powerful thing. Words can encourage or discourage, build up or tear down. As you go throughout your day today, seek to be a man whose words are like those in today's scripture. If you are in the workplace, take time to greet your coworkers with a genuine "Good morning." Be sure to truly listen for an answer when you ask, "How are you?" rather than moving on as if your question were rhetorical. You'll find that your kind words will bless you just as much as they encourage the person who receives them. You'll feel good knowing you've lifted someone's spirits or shared in that person's sorrow. You'll begin to focus on others rather than going on and on about your own problems or plans.

It has been said that conversation is an art. Hone your conversation skills this week. Be a man of encouragement, speaking words of life that remind your hearers how much they mean to you—and more importantly, to God.

*Because words have the power to affect people
deeply, it is appropriate to consider how to
encourage fellow Christians through what we say.
Words can encourage, discourage, or do nothing.*
LARRY CRABB

❖ FOR FURTHER THOUGHT:

Do you take time to greet your coworkers and people at your church? How do you think your words sound to others?

❖ PRACTICAL APPLICATION:

Practice greeting people with the same degree of genuine kindness with which you would want to be greeted. Then let this kindness spill over into other areas of your life.

---

*As a Christian, Lord, I want to make sure I come
across as genuine to everyone I meet. Help me
never sound fake, rude, or distant to those who
might need a dose of encouragement today.*

GOD'S RIGHTEOUSNESS IS GIVEN, NOT MADE

For I bear them witness that they have a zeal for
God, but not according to knowledge. For, being
ignorant of God's righteousness and going about
to establish their own righteousness, they have not
submitted themselves to the righteousness of God.

ROMANS 10:2–3

Can you make yourself more worthy of God? Is there a level of holiness you must reach before God grants you His favor?

The people of Israel were eager to please God. They committed themselves to the hard work of obedience and added an abundance of additional guidelines to make sure they were on the straightest, most narrow path. Tragically, the apostle Paul characterized them as zealous but ignorant, unaware of what God had given to them for free.

It's possible to be so committed to your own desire for God that you rebel against His path toward holiness. It can feel discouraging to realize that even with the best intentions, you've stumbled down the wrong path. Even if you mean well, God will measure your life by whether or not you've submitted to Him.

Zeal won't bring your heart any closer to God if you're headed down the wrong path. The only corrective is God's Word, read, studied, and applied. Make sure your zeal is "according to knowledge."

Whoever pursues true virtue participates in nothing other than God, because He is Himself absolute virtue.
GREGORY OF NYSSA

✤ FOR FURTHER THOUGHT:

How can you be sure you're not chasing after wrong ideas about what God really wants from you?

✤ PRACTICAL APPLICATION:

Have you ever met a person who was passionate about a false belief? How can you help that person—even if it's yourself—to see truth?

Lord, I want to be enthusiastic in my spiritual pursuits—but most importantly, I want to be chasing the right things! Give me wisdom to discern truth from error.

SERVING GOD BY SERVING OTHERS

"And the King shall answer and say to them, 'Truly
I say to you, because you have done it to one of the
least of these My brothers, you have done it to Me.'"
MATTHEW 25:40

Today's scripture (as well as some other passages like James 2:14–26) seems to imply that serving others is a requirement for salvation. That's a real head-scratcher for some Christians, who know that the Bible is clear that salvation is based on faith in Jesus alone and not on our good works.

However, when we step back and take a broader look at the entire biblical message of salvation, we see that the words of Jesus and James don't contradict this central theme at all. Instead, they teach that those who have received salvation by faith—and therefore have God's Spirit living within them—will be motivated to serve out of true love for God and others.

Doing good things for others won't earn anyone God's eternal salvation. On the other hand, any true man of God will be motivated to serve others, knowing that when he serves the "least of these," he's serving God Himself.

Do you believe God is calling you to have a bigger heart for service? Have you been wondering what kind of service He has in mind for you? Ask Him to first give you the right motivation to serve, and then ask Him to show you ways you can serve others.

The opportunities are all around you—you just have to ask and keep your eyes open.

This is true zeal for God—to know Him and love Him with a deep and consuming love, and to serve others in the same way we would serve Jesus. Anything else is an imitation.
KEITH GREEN

›› FOR FURTHER THOUGHT:

What are some ways that your faith in Christ shines through in your treatment of others?

›› PRACTICAL APPLICATION:

Is there anyone in your life whom you feel God is calling you to serve? What can you do to help?

Lord, I don't want my faith in You to be a dead faith—I want it to be a living, active faith marked by obedience and servitude. Show me how I can bless and serve others today.

BE HOLY

But as He who has called you is holy, so you
be holy in all manner of conduct, because
it is written, "Be holy, for I am holy."
1 PETER 1:15–16

In his epistle, Peter reiterates one of God's seemingly impossible commands: be holy.

God had first given the command to the nation of Israel. He emphasized it by repeating "be holy" four times in the book of Leviticus alone (11:44, 11:45, 19:2, 20:7).

The word *be* can also be translated "become." And the meaning of the word *holy* becomes clearer when we examine another command in Leviticus: "consecrate yourselves" (11:44 NIV). We are in the process of becoming holy, purifying ourselves from contaminants of body and spirit (2 Corinthians 7:11) and empowered by the refining fire of the Holy Spirit. When Christ returns, we will be like Him. That hope encourages us to dedicate ourselves to God in the here and now (1 John 3:3)—100 percent pure. No impurities (1 Thessalonians 4:7). No distractions. Just commitment to God.

We're not there yet, of course. But we will be. "He has chosen us in Him before the foundation of the world, that we should be holy and without blame before Him in love" (Ephesians 1:4).

*Do not be content with a static Christian
life. Determine rather to grow in faith
and love, in knowledge and holiness.*
JOHN STOTT

❥ FOR FURTHER THOUGHT:

Why do you think consecration (or sanctification)
is a gradual process rather than an overnight
transformation?

❥ PRACTICAL APPLICATION:

How can you measure upward progress in your own
walk with God?

---

*Father, continue making me more like
You. May I never lose sight of Your
righteousness as my ultimate goal.*

ABSOLUTE COMMITMENT

*"He who does not take his cross and follow after Me
is not worthy of Me. He who finds his life shall lose
it, and he who loses his life for My sake shall find it."*
MATTHEW 10:38–39

You've heard people say they have a "cross to bear." They're
usually referring to some burden they must endure—a hard
relationship, a chronic disease, an addiction. But the cross
really means only one thing: suffering and death. Jesus' call
to take up your cross is about dying to self, letting go of your
plans and desires, and letting God replace them with His.

This is especially difficult for those who think they're
doing God a favor by receiving Christ: *Imagine God using my
talents for the good of His kingdom!* But if they had anything
to offer God, would the cross have been necessary?

In Christ, you're reborn spiritually. But you'll bear the
burdens of the flesh until either you die or Jesus comes back.
However, whenever you share in the suffering that Christ
endured, God will redeem all your mistakes and hardships—
self-made or not. He'll turn them into bridges to others who
are experiencing similar levels of pain. It's not easy to love
people the way Jesus loves you, but it's worth it.

Commitment is the one and only way
by which we may know the Christ.
MARTIN BELL

❯ FOR FURTHER THOUGHT:

How committed would you say you are to God?
What evidence do you have to back up your answer?

❯ PRACTICAL APPLICATION:

To increase your commitment to God, practice by
improving your commitment to others. Spend more
time with your wife and kids, visit that widow who
lives down the street, or be a better friend to someone
in your church.

Lord God, thank You for committing to Your
plan to save me. The least I can do in return is to
commit my entire live in service to You and others.
Teach me how to do this moment by moment.

WALK IN LOVE

*And this is love: that we walk according
to His commandments. This is the
commandment, that, as you have heard from
the beginning, you should walk in it.*

2 JOHN 6

"Walk in love." It sounds so easy, so attractive. So why don't more people do it?

Because it goes against our worst instincts. Let's not forget we were rebels from the start. Eve, encouraged by the serpent, feared God was keeping something from her. So she went her own way—and took Adam with her. Think we are wiser today? Think again. We're all still doing our own thing—and still getting it wrong.

It's human nature to rebel when someone keeps you down, takes advantage of you, or plays you for a fool. But this is God we're talking about—not some con artist. He doesn't have anything to prove or gain. He made everything, so it's already His. To put it bluntly, you can trust Him.

So put aside those fears. If you must rebel, rebel against rebellion. God's "commandments" are simply instructions on how to walk beside Him. He calls you today to stop going your own way and start going His—only then will you know what it's like to truly walk in love.

*Moral relativism is sin in a toga. It's
selfishness and hedonism and rebellion
dressed up in philosophers' robes.*
RYAN DOBSON

❯ FOR FURTHER THOUGHT:

In what ways do you see modern culture—maybe even
yourself—rebelling against God?

❯ PRACTICAL APPLICATION:

Why do you think it's so easy for people—even
Christians—to start down this dangerous road?
How can you find the off ramp?

---

*Loving Father, I want to follow Your commands,
but it seems rebellion is baked into my DNA.
Show me how to conquer this darker side of
my mind and walk freely in Your love.*

STOP DREAMING ABOUT EASY STREET

Many are the afflictions of the righteous,
but the LORD delivers him out of them all.

PSALM 34:19

God, His principles, and life's difficulties haven't changed over time. David's psalms aren't just stories about someone who lived a long time ago. They're stories about you and your life too.

The apostle Paul said it well: "For whatever things were written formerly were written for our learning, that through patience and comfort from the scriptures we might have hope" (Romans 15:4).

The great paradox of life is that suffering and humility are necessary steps to God's best in your life. You see that in Romans 5, in James 1, in 1 Peter 1–5, and in many other scripture passages—including today's.

The promise of hardships and trials isn't a very attractive hook. In fact, it's downright countercultural. We'd much rather enjoy a nice, comfortable lifestyle free from pain and suffering. But no wish can change reality.

God's perspective is seldom heard in David's psalms. . . but His fingerprints are everywhere. Learning to recognize them there will help you see them behind the scenes in your own life, always working toward something bigger than you can see.

In the meantime, stop dreaming about Easy Street.

*We cannot make everything pleasurable and easy if
we are going to accomplish anything significant.*
BRUCE NARRAMOR

❯❯ FOR FURTHER THOUGHT:

How often does taking "the easy way out" lead
to success? Do you view your spiritual life
as any different?

❯❯ PRACTICAL APPLICATION:

How can you improve your ability to press through
trials instead of caving in?

---

*Lord, I know the life You've called me to won't
always be easy—but I'm willing to press through
anyway. I know that in the end, the rewards will
make any pain I feel right now seem trivial.*

COMFORTED AND COMFORTING

Blessed be God, even the Father of our Lord
Jesus Christ, the Father of mercies and the
God of all comfort, who comforts us in all our
tribulation, that we may be able to comfort those
who are in any trouble, by the comfort with
which we ourselves are comforted by God. For
as the sufferings of Christ abound in us, so our
consolation also abounds through Christ.
2 CORINTHIANS 1:3–5

Young children find comfort in a pacifier, a stuffed animal, or a special blanket. But as we grow older, comfort is harder to find. Maybe a roaring fireplace or a juicy cheeseburger brings comfort from certain troubles. A talk with a friend may lighten the load on your heart. But God calls you to the source of *real* comfort: a relationship with Him.

No matter what trouble you are facing today, God is there to comfort you. You can rest in Jesus. You can come to Him and lay down your concerns. You can talk with Him, listen to Him, say back to Him the promises He makes in scripture. There is power and peace to be found in simply speaking His name.

When you can find comfort in the Lord, you are better equipped to comfort others. You can empathize with anyone who is experiencing a similar hurt. You are ready to comfort because you have been comforted.

*You will never have true pleasure or peace or
joy or comfort until you have found Christ.*
D. L. MOODY

❖ FOR FURTHER THOUGHT:

What are some ways in which God uses tragedy for
our own good and to magnify His name?

❖ PRACTICAL APPLICATION:

The next time any trial or tragedy strikes, make a
conscious decision to turn to God first.

---

*Father God, I know You've called me to
take comfort in You above all else. When
life grows burdensome, remind me of Your
goodness that never changes or disappears.*

HANDLING ANGER PROPERLY

A fool utters all his mind, but a wise
man keeps it in until afterward.
PROVERBS 29:11

This may come as a surprise to some Christian men, but the Bible teaches that anger isn't necessarily a sin. God Himself expressed His anger in scripture (see Psalm 7:11; Mark 3:5). And the apostle Paul made a distinction between anger and *sinful* anger when he wrote, "Be angry and do not sin. Don't let the sun go down on your wrath" (Ephesians 4:26).

Godly anger—also known as righteous indignation—can motivate men to glorify God and further His kingdom. It moves you to defend those who are being wronged or mistreated and to stand up for a biblical principle you see being violated.

But sinful anger, the kind of anger that moves you to contend for your own selfish desires, can damage relationships, cause unneeded pain to those you love, and hurt your witness for Christ.

Anger will come—it's just a part of life. But when you feel that emotion rising up within you, stop and ask yourself if the way you're considering expressing that anger will hurt others or displease your Father in heaven. If the answer to that question is yes, then patiently hold your words in check and choose to find a healthier, more godly way to express how you feel.

When anger wins, love always loses.
WILLARD HARLEY JR.

» FOR FURTHER THOUGHT:

Have you ever been angry for the right reason, but lashed out in the wrong way? If so, how effective (or ineffective) was your response?

» PRACTICAL APPLICATION:

Godly anger can sometimes come across as mere rage. How can we as Christians prevent this from happening?

Lord, it's so easy for me to simply lash out at sin and careless behavior, but I know You've called me to more. Show me how to dilute my anger— even the righteous kind—with Your love.

GOD-INSPIRED OPTIMISM

*"And Moses swore on that day, saying, "'Surely the land in which your feet have trampled shall be your inheritance and your children's forever, because you have wholly followed the L*ORD *my God.' . . . . If the L*ORD *will be with me, then I shall be able to drive them out as the L*ORD *said."*

JOSHUA 14:9, 12

A negative spirit is always a mark of self-reliance. To follow God wholeheartedly, as Caleb did, requires an unwavering trust in God's encouragement and empowerment. Along with that comes a confident optimism in God's presence and power in our lives—an eagerness to engage with God in His mission.

Caleb, forty-five years earlier, exuded this confident optimism. And now, at age eighty-five, he welcomed the challenge to engage in battle against the Anakites.

"Been there, done that" never entered Caleb's lexicon. He refused to leave the battle for the young men of his clan. Seeing the finish line of the race that he started decades earlier, he redoubled his effort and charged into the hill country, confident in *God's* ability, not his own. Imagine the Anakites shaking in their size 25 boots as Caleb approached, weapons drawn. They never stood a chance in the face of Caleb's divinely empowered onslaught.

Are there challenges you've been waiting years to accomplish? Are you ready to reengage, confident that you're living up to God's high calling?

Caleb's story was still being told years later (Judges 1:20). This is the very definition of the "prosperous and successful" promise of Joshua 1:8. Follow Caleb's example of faith. . .and leave a legacy worthy of God's warriors.

The pessimist sees a difficulty in every opportunity;
the optimist sees an opportunity in every difficulty.
TED ENGSTROM

❯ FOR FURTHER THOUGHT:

Are you eager to challenge yourself and see where God's plan takes you? Or are you hesitant, scared of taking that step and possibly getting hurt?

❯ PRACTICAL APPLICATION:

What scriptures can you use to build up optimism whenever you're confronted with a hard assignment from God?

I'm not content to stay in one place spiritually,
God. Give me the optimism to see the potential
in every challenge, the faith to know You have it
under control, and the courage to take the plunge.

FREEDOM TO SERVE OTHERS

And Joseph, who was surnamed Barnabas
by the apostles (which is, being interpreted,
the son of consolation), a Levite from the
country of Cyprus, having land, sold it and
brought the money and laid it at the apostles' feet.
ACTS 4:36–37

Barnabas emerged as one of the most important missionaries in the book of Acts—he joined Paul's gospel journeys, stood by John Mark in his time of failure, and worked tirelessly to share the good news of Jesus.

The first mention of Barnabas reveals something significant: he sold his field to generously provide for the needs of the poor. Before setting out on his missionary work, he unburdened himself of his field to become a worker in God's harvest. While we can't say for sure how much of a burden that field had been for Barnabas, there's no doubt that selling it freed him to serve others.

Is it possible that something you own is keeping you from clearly seeing God's calling or from taking a step of faith? There's nothing wrong with owning a field or many other things, but the burden of wealth can obscure what God wants to accomplish in your life.

Today, ask God if He wants you to free yourself of something you own so that you can better serve Him. . .and others.

Before anything that is truly of God can be born, your own preferences have to die.
ED STETZER AND DAVID PUTMAN

⇥ FOR FURTHER THOUGHT:

Have you ever hung on to a good thing so tightly that it became no longer good for you?

⇥ PRACTICAL APPLICATION:

At what point should you decide to let something go in exchange for greater freedom to serve God?

Lord Jesus, I'm very grateful for all the blessings I know I don't deserve. However, I never want any of these good things to stand in the way of Your best calling. Teach me the art of surrender.

GOD EMPOWERS

Saul answered and said, "Am I not a Benjamite,
of the smallest of the tribes of Israel? And is not
my family the least of all the families of the tribe
of Benjamin? Why then do you speak so to me?"

1 SAMUEL 9:21

Saul's father, Kish, was a wealthy, influential man. And Saul was known for being the most handsome male in Israel (1 Samuel 9:1–2). But when he considered his tribe's heritage—they were the smallest tribe in Israel after being decimated in a civil war (Judges 20)—he couldn't understand why Samuel had pointed to Saul and his family as the focus of all Israel's hopes (1 Samuel 9:20).

We aren't told why Saul considered his family to be the least important in his small tribe. Maybe he was naturally humble. Maybe he was overwhelmed to think that his nation's hopes would fall on his shoulders. At this point, Saul didn't seem to understand that God was behind him—or that after Samuel anointed him as king, God would give Saul a new heart (1 Samuel 10:9).

The time may come when *you* are approached with an opportunity to serve. Will you respond like Saul, with a laundry list of reasons why you aren't able? Or will you consider the possibility that God is calling you to a new ministry? If the latter, be sure of this: God will empower you to perform the job.

*We must understand that the Holy Spirit
lives in us to empower us to succeed
at whatever God calls us to do.*
T. D. JAKES

❯❯ FOR FURTHER THOUGHT:

Has God ever presented you with a golden opportunity
to step outside of your comfort zone and help
someone? If so, how did you respond?

❯❯ PRACTICAL APPLICATION:

Use your success (or failure) in that situation as a guide
for how you should handle the next.

---

*Father, I know You've called me to live a life of
constant trust and servitude. May I always be
attentive to Your leading, never so closed-minded
that I miss the gentle leading of Your voice.*

PUT ON JESUS CHRIST

*But put on the Lord Jesus Christ, and do not
make provision for the flesh, to fulfill its lusts.*
ROMANS 13:14

In today's passage, the apostle Paul provides a one-two punch for living the victorious Christian life. First, he doesn't tell the Christian to stand strong in his own strength, but rather to "put on the Lord Jesus Christ." That means taking on His ways and espousing His views. Second, the Christian is to make no provision for the flesh. The Greek word rendered "provision" here means "forethought."

Are you minding your spirit, making it a priority to put on Jesus Christ every hour of the day? If so, what specific steps are you taking to smash provisions for the flesh? Do you need to unsubscribe to a certain cable channel? Attend meetings to help you stay sober? Talk to somebody about your jealous streak? Start an anger management recovery program?

According to Romans 13:13, the sins of the flesh include drunkenness, sexual immorality, sensuality, quarreling, and jealousy. You know your areas of weakness. God is calling you to go on the offensive and take decisive action against them.

*The mortification of indwelling sin remaining
in our mortal bodies, that it may not have life
and power to bring forth the works or deeds of
the flesh, is the constant duty of believers.*

JOHN OWEN

❯ FOR FURTHER THOUGHT:

The word *flesh* is often used in the Bible to describe
sinfulness. Why?

❯ PRACTICAL APPLICATION:

In what ways do the spiritual and the physical clash in
your own life? How can you help your spiritual side to
victory?

---

*Lord, I'm just a man, so I sometimes get
caught up in fleshly desires and activities.
Show me the better life You've called me
to, and then give me the willpower to
pursue that life with all I have.*

LET IT PASS

He who covers a transgression seeks love,
but he who repeats a matter separates friends.
PROVERBS 17:9

We all know *that guy*—the one who's always scarfing up the last donut (his third) without asking whether you've had one yet. Or maybe the guy who borrows a valuable tool and loses it. . .then says he can't afford to replace it now. And you need it for work on Monday.

How do you respond?

Hopefully, the donut is a nonissue. It is, after all, a rather minor offense. But what about the more hurtful words and the larger losses—especially those that keep happening? Are those worth losing a friend over? Probably not.

You can still express your disappointment and calmly let him know how this makes you feel. And you probably should express your emotions. But it's not wise to hold a grudge. Leviticus 19:18 says, "You shall not. . .bear any grudge against the children of your people, but you shall love your neighbor as yourself." Love is the whole reason why grudges are a bad idea.

God calls you to take His commands seriously at all times—both in your everyday life and in the workplace. They may not be easy to implement, but they're guaranteed to work.

Bitterness is paralysis.
DAVID AUGSBURGER

✦ FOR FURTHER THOUGHT:

Why is bitterness so damaging to the Christian life?

✦ PRACTICAL APPLICATION:

The next time someone annoys you, force yourself to remember a time when you behaved in the same way toward someone else. Then respond to that person with the same degree of understanding which you'd show to that prior version of yourself.

---

*Thank You, Father, for not holding a
grudge against me—even when I deserve it.
Show me how to trade in my bitterness for Your love.*

LISTEN TO THE SILENCE

And [Jesus] said to them, "He who
has ears to hear, let him hear."
MARK 4:9

On a still, winter night in the country, the silence is almost uncanny. The nearly complete lack of noise somehow clears the mind and points us to deeper thoughts.

We think we know what silence is, but most of us are automatically tuning out the noise of distant traffic, the heating system, and even the television and radio each second.

Sadly, it's easy to do the same thing in our Christian life. We "tune out" the little sins that creep into our day, and we think we're doing all right. But when we're truly silent before God, those little sins cry out like a chainsaw on a country evening—a shock that compels us to do something about them.

God calls you to find some real silence, which refreshes the soul. Without any other distractions, spend some time listening to Him. "Hear" what God has to say specifically to you—and grow into the man He wants you to be.

*It is in lonely solitude that God
delivers His best thoughts.*
CHARLES SWINDOLL

⇢ FOR FURTHER THOUGHT:

When is the last time you truly waited in silence for
God's voice? How did it turn out?

⇢ PRACTICAL APPLICATION:

Do you know of any places—a lakeside, barn, or even
closet—that are perfect for listening to God? When
can you get there?

---

*Lord, I'm a busy man. Teach me how to
slow down once in a while and wait for
You to speak. I never want the business of
the day to cause me to miss Your voice.*

PROVE YOURSELF A MAN

"I am going the way of all the earth. Therefore
be strong, and prove yourself a man."
1 Kings 2:2

At the end of David's life, he charged his son Solomon to prove himself a man. Solomon would need to be wise as he assumed the role of king. Even though he was young, he would need to act much older. David explained what that would look like: "And keep the charge of the LORD your God, to walk in His ways, to keep His statutes and His commandments and His judgments and His testimonies, as it is written in the law of Moses, that you may prosper in all that you do and wherever you turn" (1 Kings 2:3).

Sadly, Solomon wasn't always successful. While he was indeed wise, he "loved many foreign women" (1 Kings 11:1), and eventually, "his wives turned away his heart after other gods. And his heart was not perfect with the LORD his God" (verse 4). He also gathered many possessions (Ecclesiastes 2:7) and indulged in wine (Ecclesiastes 2:3) in search of fulfillment. Eventually, he lamented his failures, saying: "Then I looked at all the works that my hands had done, and on the labor that I had labored to do, and behold, all was vanity and vexation of spirit, and there was no profit under the sun" (Ecclesiastes 2:11).

If even the wisest of men can be turned against the Lord by his baser appetites, how much more can we? Don't try to go it alone—admit your struggles to God and seek out a Christian friend to hold you accountable.

Let your resolve be that, by the grace of God enabling you, you will cultivate moral refinement, and everything that can truly exalt and ennoble character; and nothing whatever is there in your position in life, or the circumstances with which you are surrounded, to hinder you from carrying out this resolution.
JOHN DAWSON

❯ FOR FURTHER THOUGHT:

What are some of the most common things that turn Christian men from God?

❯ PRACTICAL APPLICATION:

How can you—with God's help—take steps to ensure you don't fall into the same trap?

Lord, I see distractions all around me, but I know You call me to rise above these temporal pleasures in pursuit of Your eternal glory. Grant me the resolve to stay on this narrow path.

OVERCOMING SIN

Your word have I hidden in my heart,
that I might not sin against You.
PSALM 119:11

The great nineteenth-century American evangelist Dwight L. Moody said, "The Bible will keep you from sin, or sin will keep you from the Bible."

The writer of Psalm 119 would heartily agree. In today's scripture, he declared that he kept his heart and mind focused on the Word of God so that he could avoid sinning against his God. The same thing can be true for you today.

The writer of the epistle to the Hebrews wrote this of the Bible's power: "For the word of God is living and powerful and sharper than any two-edged sword, piercing even to the dividing of soul and spirit, and of the joints and marrow, and is a discerner of the thoughts and intentions of the heart" (Hebrews 4:12).

Sadly, too many Christians don't make sufficient use of what the apostle Paul called "the sword of the Spirit" (Ephesians 6:17)—and that results in weak, powerless lives. But if you can learn to walk in the tremendous power the Bible gives you to live an overcoming life, you'll find it possible to say yes to the things that please God and no to the things that don't.

Make it your goal to learn to wield this mighty sword by reading God's Word, memorizing it, and meditating on it.

Believers who don't live with a scheduled diet of
God's Word will fail to stay competitive spiritually.
TONY EVANS AND JONATHAN EVANS

❯❯ FOR FURTHER THOUGHT:

What Bible passages do you feel apply most to your everyday life?

❯❯ PRACTICAL APPLICATION:

Use whatever tactic works best for you—index cards, repetition, self-made quizzes, or a combination of all three—to memorize those sections of God's Word.

---

*God, I know You've called me to be a diligent
student of Your Word, so I don't want to live
each day ignorant about what it truly says.
Show me how to anchor my life to its words.*

STRENGTH IN SURRENDER

Finally, my brothers, be strong in the
Lord and in the power of His might.
Ephesians 6:10

Men, generally speaking, like to be in control. From earliest childhood, we like to say, "I can do it myself!" All through life, we want to impress others with our own strength—physical, emotional, intellectual, and even spiritual. But God's ways are often very different than ours (see Isaiah 55:8). He calls us to surrender.

God does assign certain tasks to us, giving us areas of responsibility. We are expected to do our best, develop our gifts, and accomplish as much as we can for His glory. But we are never in total control. Our strength comes from God, from the power of *His* might. Many centuries before the apostle Paul wrote to the Ephesians, Moses told the ancient Israelites, "You shall remember the Lord your God, for it is He who gives you power to get wealth" (Deuteronomy 8:18).

Christians walk a fine line. We are supposed to work. We are called to be strong. But the strength for our work always comes from God, and He gives that strength as we surrender to Him. Surrendering is choosing to obey or follow someone other than yourself. As Paul wrote elsewhere, "Do you not know that the one to whom you yield yourselves as servants to obey, you are his servants to whom you obey, whether of sin to death, or of obedience to righteousness?" (Romans 6:16). Our strength comes from choosing to follow Christ.

*True greatness is found in simple
surrender to God's plan for our lives.*
JIM CYMBALA

❖ FOR FURTHER THOUGHT:

When things don't go your way, what is your response?
Do you become angry and impatient, or do you sit
back and trust that God knows best?

❖ PRACTICAL APPLICATION:

How can you relinquish your desire for control and
commit yourself to following wherever God leads?

---

*Father, I give up whatever control that I used to
think I have. My life is in Your hands—use me
in whatever way brings the most glory to You.*

HOME SWEET HOME?

While we are at home in the body
we are absent from the Lord.
2 Corinthians 5:6

In 2 Corinthians 5:1–10, Paul was speaking about his struggle between life and death. He realized that in some ways, this physical life kept him from being "at home" with the Lord.

There is no doubt about it—our planet is the one place in the universe where life flourishes. We were made for this place. More precisely, this world was created for us (Genesis 1:26–27). We are "at home" here.

But this world as it now exists is not our *true* home. We were never meant for this sin-ravaged and broken planet. We were never meant to experience the suffering and sadness of a cursed world. We were meant to enjoy intimacy with God without any barriers (Genesis 3).

Being "at home" also means being in a place where we feel comfortable, at rest, and at ease. So Paul's comment really means that the more comfortable we are here—the more at home we feel in our sinful culture—the farther we are from being at home with Christ.

We should not be "at home" in this world's sinful atmosphere. Instead, God calls us to be restless—never content until we are truly "at home" with Christ.

Thou hast made us for Thyself, O Lord,
and our hearts are restless until they rest in Thee.
AUGUSTINE

» FOR FURTHER THOUGHT:

What are some methods that our culture uses to pull our focus down from heaven and onto earth? Which are the most effective?

» PRACTICAL APPLICATION:

How effective have culture's tactics been on you? How can you combat this perpetual tug and make sure your allegiance still lies with God?

Heavenly Father, keep me to be uncomfortable.
May I never settle into the rut of sin, so complacent
that I forget why I'm here. Constantly remind me
of the true purpose for which You've called me.

WITH HIM

Oh that men would praise the LORD for His goodness
and for His wonderful works to the children of men!

PSALM 107:15

Have you ever felt like your job doesn't matter?

Here are some of the jobs assigned in Old Testament times: "Twenty-four thousand were to oversee the work of the house of the LORD. . . . Four thousand were gatekeepers" (1 Chronicles 23:4–5). At times even the military commanders had to stop leading their troops to help choose workers "who should prophesy with harps, with lyres, and with cymbals" (1 Chronicles 25:1). Although these routines certainly had moments of meaning, there had to have been days when repairing building damage, scrubbing bowls, listening to complaining employees, and practicing musical instruments seemed patronizing and pointless.

In New Testament times, some people invited popular leaders like Paul and Apollos to their homes (Acts 18:26), while others spent long months accompanying Paul to discussions in the lecture hall of Tyrannus (19:9–10). How did these individuals make such moments meaningful?

Perhaps they spent these unrewarded and unrecognized hours remembering the one who brought them out of darkness. Maybe they learned to spend less time comparing and more time praising the Lord "for His goodness and for His wonderful works to the children of men" (Psalm 107:15).

Happiness comes in knowing you are working with God.

I've come to the conclusion that I would rather
labor in obscurity for God than be famous for
doing something insignificant with my life.
RORY NOLAND

❯ FOR FURTHER THOUGHT:

When you have done a kindness for someone, are you eager to tell others or are you content to let these deeds slide by unnoticed?

❯ PRACTICAL APPLICATION:

The next time you feel the urge to brag on yourself, be honest with God about your feelings—then try replacing the word *I* with *God*.

Lord God, I know that all of my good deeds stem
from Your grace. Show me how to find contentment
in the purpose of my work—not in the work itself.

NO MORE PRETENSE

Therefore, putting away lying, speak truth every man
with his neighbor, for we are members of one another.
EPHESIANS 4:25

Our natural inclination is to present our best. . .while hiding the rest. We smile, even though we are feeling down. We nod our head in agreement during a Bible study or sermon, even though we don't understand. We pray in the company of others, even when our private prayer life is nonexistent.

In the verse above, the apostle Paul calls for an end to pretense in the church. He isn't necessarily saying we should wear our heart on our sleeve, shake our head in disagreement at biblical teaching, or refuse to pray in the company of others if we've failed to do so at home. But he is saying that pretense comes with a cost. When we lie to one another, openly or subtly, we harm not only others but ourselves.

Consider your own small group of Christian fellowship. Can you see pretense in others? How has this affected your relationships within the group? How has it affected your ability to minister to one another? If you can see pretense in them, they can probably see it in you too. Resolve to tell them the truth, knowing it will make the ground fertile for ministry.

O brethren, above all things shun hypocrisy.
If ye mean to be damned, make up your minds
to it, and be damned like honest men; but do
not, I beseech you, pretend to go to heaven
while all the time you are going to hell.
CHARLES SPURGEON

❯ FOR FURTHER THOUGHT:

Why is it so hard for a Christian man to be honest
about his failures?

❯ PRACTICAL APPLICATION:

To begin with the process of vanquishing pretense,
be honest with someone today. Tell a trusted friend
about a mistake you've made or a flaw you have. If that
person is truly a friend, he will commend you for your
honesty rather than judge you.

Father, I might be great at not lying with my
words—but lying with my actions comes a little
more easily. Show me how to be honest in every
aspect of my life, even if it's painful or hard.

CALLED TO LET GO

"He who loves his life shall lose it, and he who
hates his life in this world shall keep it to eternal
life. If any man serves Me, let him follow Me.
And where I am, there My servant shall be also.
If any man serves Me, My Father will honor him."
JOHN 12:25–26

There is nothing in this life you can keep or take with you into eternity other than what springs from your love for God. Your obedience and selfless service to others demonstrates your faith in God and your confidence in the life to come.

Trading your soul for what you can gain for yourself today is a bad trade. The more you concentrate on accumulating in this world, the less capacity you'll have to hold on to what God cares about the most.

Think of the attachments to this world—whether emotional, relational, or physical—that hold you back from a closer walk with God. They are burdens that keep you from the only prize that matters.

The more you surrender to God, the less you have to worry about defending. The more you've emptied from your life, the better prepared you are to receive what God wants to give you.

There must be no dallying with an attachment
which is incompatible with the love of God.
FRANCIS DE SALES

✦ FOR FURTHER THOUGHT:

What are some examples of things that interfere with
a man's walk with God? How many of these items are
necessarily bad?

✦ PRACTICAL APPLICATION:

Is there anything in your life—a person, a possession,
an activity—that is getting between you and your time
with God? If so, how can you take steps to diminish or
remove these distractions?

Father, You are the most important goal in
the universe. Give me the determination and
focus to keep my spiritual eyes solely on You.
Nothing else holds a candle to Your glory.

STRENGTH IN WEAKNESS

Therefore I take pleasure in weaknesses, in reproaches, in necessities, in persecutions, in distresses, for Christ's sake. For when I am weak, then I am strong.

2 CORINTHIANS 12:10

It isn't natural—especially for men—to be content with weakness. And when others see our weaknesses, we likely feel shame or even anger. These feelings may cause us to question our usefulness to Christ. After all, how can God use someone who keeps falling into sin?

In his second letter to the Corinthians, the apostle Paul mentions a weakness of his own. No one knows exactly what Paul meant when he said that he was given a "thorn in the flesh," but it is clear that Satan used this weakness to attack Paul.

Three times, Paul asked God to remove this weakness, but God responded, "My grace is sufficient for you, for My strength is made perfect in weakness" (2 Corinthians 12:9).

No matter what weaknesses you have, what insults you endure, what hardships you live through, God calls you to remember that His grace is sufficient. Stop trying to overcome your weakness with your own strength; instead, allow God to work in you. And once others see your example of weakness transformed, they'll have reason to praise God instead of you.

Your biggest weakness is God's greatest opportunity.
CHARLES STANLEY

❖ FOR FURTHER THOUGHT:

What is your "thorn in the flesh"? A temptation?
A physical weakness? A negative attitude?

❖ PRACTICAL APPLICATION:

When you pray, start thanking God for your "thorn,"
knowing that He's using it to magnify His own glory
through you. Then make sure you're willing to let Him.

---

*Lord, I know I'm an imperfect man—but You are
a perfect God. Thank You for using the ashes of my
failures to help build Your glorious kingdom.*

WORSHIP LIKE A MAN

*And David danced before the LORD with
all his might, and David was girded with a
linen ephod. So David and all the house of
Israel brought up the ark of the LORD with
shouting and with the sound of the trumpet.*

2 SAMUEL 6:14–15

Masculinity is made complete in worship. Where else can
a man open himself so completely without fear of failure,
without pretending to be strong or competent or in control?
Where else can a man be so honest without fear of being
taken advantage of? Where else can a man look into the
face of the Realest Man of All?

To worship as a man means to disdain what others
think of your openness. When his wife, Michal, daughter
of Saul, rebuked him for this enthusiastic public display,
he responded: "It was before the LORD, who chose me
before your father and before all his house, to appoint me
ruler over the people of the LORD, over Israel. Therefore I
will dance before the LORD" (2 Samuel 6:21).

Basically, David didn't give a rip what people thought
of him when he worshipped. David cared only for God's
opinion. As a shepherd/warrior/king, he had faced death
from man and beast, so public opinion wasn't about to scare
him away from worshipping with all his might.

To humble yourself in worship—confessing, singing,

crying, dancing with wild abandon before your God—is to
return to masculinity, not to relinquish it.

God will refuse to accept worship that is halfhearted
or less than what he deserves. Worship that requires
little of us is likewise worth little to God.
HENRY AND TOM BLACKABY

›› FOR FURTHER THOUGHT:

What does "true" worship look like to you? How does
this image line up with the Bible's definition?

›› PRACTICAL APPLICATION:

The next time you sing songs of worship at church,
dwell on the meaning of the words—not on the
rhythm or the sound of your voice. Then think of
yourself as speaking these words directly to God.
After all, you are!

Lord, You've called me to a life of worship.
Please help me overcome my natural inhibitions
so that I can praise You in the purest way possible.

WATCH, PRAY, WIN

But Jonah rose up to flee to Tarshish
from the presence of the LORD.
JONAH 1:3

What's the story of Jonah really about? That you should always wear a life jacket? Try again. That you should always obey God? Ultimately, yes. But there's another, more subtle lesson in this brief Old Testament book: the need to fight temptation in our lives.

God gave Jonah a clear command. . .and Jonah immediately wanted to disobey. He wasn't alone—everyone struggles with that temptation. And though it's not easy to overcome these emotions, it isn't impossible either—as long as we rely on God's strength. Notice what the apostle Paul said in 1 Corinthians 10:13: "God is faithful, who will not allow you to be tempted above what you are able, but with the temptation *will also make a way of escape*" (emphasis added).

How can you find that way out? Jesus calls you to "watch and pray, lest you enter into temptation" (Mark 14:38). No special skill required, just willingness. Can you commit to watching and praying today?

*Temptation is around us every day. It doesn't
usually lurk in the bushes for a surprise attack.
Instead it slowly befriends us, convincing
us that we have nothing to fear.*
GREGG MATTE

❯ FOR FURTHER THOUGHT:

What does it take to escape temptation? If a Christian
man is willing to escape, do you think God leaves him
to himself or assists him?

❯ PRACTICAL APPLICATION:

When you're tempted, how often do you actively
seek—and find—God's escape route? What physical
pursuits might help you avoid spiritual temptations?

---

*Thank You, Father, for offering a way out of every
temptation. Teach me to take this escape route
every time—I never want to abuse Your grace.*

KNOW YOUR WORTH

"But He knows the way that I take. When He has tested me, I shall come forth as gold."

JOB 23:10

In the temple treasury, Jesus pointed out a poor widow who had quietly contributed two very small bronze coins. Her gift demonstrated her implicit trust in God's ability to supply all her needs. The widow's mites were worth far more than everything the rich had donated (Mark 12:41–44). Even when you can't afford it, trust God and give.

In one of His parables, Jesus talked about a wealthy farmer who'd laid up enough to retire. He was quite proud of his accomplishments. Little did he know, however, that he would die that very night (Luke 12:16–21). Never trust earthly wealth.

In two short parables, Jesus said it was worth selling everything you have to obtain the kingdom of heaven. The kingdom of God is worth more than all your accumulated wealth here on earth (Matthew 13:44–46). Buy it.

In Matthew 6:26 and 10:29–31 and Luke 12:6–7, Jesus pointed out that since God cares so much for the birds, He values us much more. Receive His love.

In Matthew 16:26 and Mark 8:36–37, Jesus says the world's vast wealth is nothing compared to the value of your soul. Give it to God.

*Think of the worth of a single soul—a soul delivered
from eternal death, and made an heir of eternal bliss!*
WILLIAM CAREY

›› FOR FURTHER THOUGHT:

Which do you think is more effective: following a
mere checklist—tithing, church attendance, and daily
Bible reading—or dipping deeper into your resources,
giving until it hurts?

›› PRACTICAL QUESTION:

How are you giving God what He deserves?

---

*Lord, it's sometimes tempting to think that since
salvation is free, I don't have to do anything.
But I know You've called me to more. Show me
how to give all I have for Your kingdom.*

WHEN OTHERS SPEAK WELL OF YOU

"Son of man, say to the prince of Tyre, 'This is what the Lord GOD says: "Because your heart is lifted up and you have said, 'I am a god; I sit in the seat of God, in the midst of the seas' (yet you are a man, and not God, though you set your heart as the heart of God). . ."' "

EZEKIEL 28:2

The king of Tyre was a talented and wise leader who built his city into one of the richest, most beautiful cities in the world. Sadly, though, the king allowed the praises of others to fill him with extreme pride. He began to see himself as a god and not as a mere man.

One of the biggest potential dangers in accomplishing great things—as a leader, businessman, or minister—is the praise people heap on you. If you're not careful, their words can go to your head and cause you to think more highly of yourself than you should.

It happened to the king of Tyre. It can happen to anyone.

When people compliment you, respond graciously. But God calls you to go beyond that—to remind yourself that He alone deserves all the credit for who you are and what you do.

Catch [a man] at the moment when he is really poor in spirit and smuggle into his mind the gratifying reflection, "By jove! I'm being humble," and almost immediately pride—pride at his own humility—will appear.
C. S. LEWIS

❖ FOR FURTHER THOUGHT:

Who do you know with an ego problem? Is pride ever an issue for you?

❖ PRACTICAL APPLICATION:

The next time you feel tempted to brag on yourself, make a mental list of all the things outside your control that led you to that point. Then turn your pride into thankfulness toward the God who leads your life.

Thank You, Lord, for giving me the ability to serve You. Let me never think this ability came about from my own power; instead, show me how to point others to You with every action I take.

STANDING IN THE GAP

"And I sought for a man among them who should make up the hedge and stand in the gap before Me for the land, that I should not destroy it. But I found none."

Ezekiel 22:30

Do you ever look around and wonder if humanity is a lost cause? Have you ever seen someone you thought was beyond the reach of God Himself?

Your very human reaction might be to give up and let things take their course. Today's verse is God's challenge to Christian men who know how desperately their nation—and the rest of the world—needs God's mercy.

God loves changing hearts when one of His people chooses to "stand in the gap" on behalf of an individual, a group of people, or even a whole nation. This is what the term "intercessory prayer" means—praying on behalf of others, knowing that God desires to show mercy and grace, even when a situation looks hopeless.

Are you willing to stand in the gap today? Are you willing to pray over and over again for someone you know who needs God's loving touch?

When people love one another, they pray for one another, and when they pray for one another they learn to love one another more deeply.
GLENN DAMAN

❖ FOR FURTHER THOUGHT:

Why do you think God wants us to "stand in the gap" for others?

❖ PRACTICAL SUGGESTION:

Who can you stand in the gap for today?

Father, it's easy to look down on others. But I know You call me to a greater path—a path of compassion, empathy, and prayer on their behalf. Show me how to take this path each day.

FIRST THINGS FIRST

But Jesus said to him, "Follow Me,
and let the dead bury their dead."
MATTHEW 8:22

Part of being a responsible adult is making plans and following through on commitments. Take a moment and think of all the things you've done in the past week. . .and all the things on tap for this week. Once your head stops spinning, think of how often you deliberately brought God into those plans. Then ask yourself, *Is this God's best for me?*

Trusting God includes trusting His timing. Life is ridiculously busy, and between work and family needs and church activities, it's easy to reach a level of unrealistic expectation and spiritual exhaustion. We begin to think that just because we're doing the best we can, God's schedule is going to fit into our own. But that's not necessarily true. Stay focused on God, not the tyranny of the urgent.

Are you willing to let God interrupt your plans? Part of being His son means a willingness to slow down, ask Him for perspective, and trust that His interruptions are for your ultimate benefit.

God will never adjust His agenda to fit ours.
He will not speed up His pace to catch up with ours;
we need to slow our pace in order to recover our
walk with Him. God will not scream and shout
over the noisy clamor; He expects us to seek quietness,
where His still small voice can be heard again.
CHARLES SWINDOLL

❯❯ FOR FURTHER THOUGHT:

When you're having a busy day, do you ever make a conscious effort to listen for God's voice?

❯❯ PRACTICAL APPLICATION:

The next time something inside you tells you to slow down, pray, or even dwell on God's mercy, don't pass up this divine opportunity.

Lord God, I don't want to be so busy with
trivialities that I miss out on the single most
important thing in life: Your voice. Show me how
to be more spiritually attentive each moment.

CITIZENS OF HEAVEN

*For our citizenship is in heaven, from where we
also look for the Savior, the Lord Jesus Christ.*

PHILIPPIANS 3:20

In this passage, the Greek word rendered "citizenship" is broad in its translation, indicating our citizenship, thoughts, and affections are already in heaven.

For every Christian, heaven is home. From the moment you accept Christ, you are adopted into God's family with the promise of spending eternity with Him and all the saints who have gone before you. You are no longer a citizen of this earth; you are born from above, and your name is written in God's celestial register.

Because your citizenship is in heaven, so are your hopes, thoughts, and affections. You are *in* the world, but not *of* it any longer. The book of Hebrews says that Abraham and his descendants "looked for a city that has foundations, whose builder and maker is God" (11:10). They considered themselves strangers on this earth because they desired "a better country—that is, a heavenly one" (11:16).

As a citizen of heaven, you can enjoy all the rights and privileges of your heavenly Father. Meanwhile, remember to look to Jesus and stay steadfast in His Word until He ushers you home.

The fact that we have our citizenship in heaven ought to make us better citizens on earth, no matter under what form of government we may live.
WARREN WIERSBE

›› FOR FURTHER THOUGHT:

How does being a citizen of heaven yet a resident of earth lead to lifelong tension? In what areas of life does this tension reveal itself the most?

›› PRACTICAL APPLICATION:

How do your thoughts, attitudes, and actions show signs of your dual citizenship? How could they do that better?

Father, I know my true citizenship lies in heaven, yet I'm often distracted by where I am right now. Show me how to let my destination influence my current choices—and not vice versa.

DO YOU NEED AN OUTSIDE PERSPECTIVE?

"I have not troubled Israel, but you and
your father's house have, in that you have
forsaken the commandments of the LORD
and you have followed the Baals."

1 KINGS 18:18

Ahab was more than ready to transfer the blame for his troubles onto Elijah. Rather than examining his actions and taking ownership for the ways he had abandoned God's laws, it was much easier for the king to point a finger at the messenger.

When you're going through an uncertain time, it's quite difficult to step back and see the highs and lows with clarity. But an outside perspective, like Elijah's, can cut to the chase in an instant, offering a point of view that slices through any doubts, debates, or attempts to minimize your actions.

Relying on someone for wisdom and guidance isn't easy. It means becoming vulnerable and recognizing that someone else has your best interests in mind. It's much easier to blame the messenger instead. Yet God calls you to take that step of faith, to seek the help of a trusted friend or mentor. And once you see matters as they truly are and act accordingly, you'll find new freedom and life in the most unlikely of places.

*Focusing on difficulties intensifies and enlarges
the problem. When we focus our attention
on God, the problem is put into its proper
perspective and it no longer overwhelms us.*
CHARLES STANLEY

❯❯ FOR FURTHER THOUGHT:

How might a proper perspective on life improve a
Christian man's behavior when life gets stressful?

❯❯ PRACTICAL APPLICATION:

Commit to hearing feedback, even criticism, when it's
offered. If the information is false, you don't lose
anything. If it's true, it may help you tremendously.

---

*Lord, life can be strenuous and emotionally
taxing sometimes. Thank You for offering a
perspective that allows me to look past the pain
and toward a brighter future with You.*

FLEE FROM HER

*I find more bitter than death the woman whose
heart is snares and nets, and her hands like
chains. Whoever pleases God shall escape from
her, but the sinner shall be taken by her.*

ECCLESIASTES 7:26

If any man was qualified to warn other men about seduction, it would be Solomon. He had seven hundred wives and three hundred concubines, and they turned his heart away from the Lord to worship Ashtoreth and Molech (1 Kings 11:3–5). "And Solomon did evil in the sight of the LORD and did not go fully after the LORD, as his father, David, did" (1 Kings 11:6).

If you could take a peek at what God has recorded about your dealings with worldly women, what might it say? Would it say you've been pleasing to Him by escaping such snares? Or would it say their soft hands were like chains, binding you and keeping you from walking in the Spirit as you ought?

God calls you to escape the seductress before she turns your heart away from God. It's not too late. Draw upon God's power and run.

*Lust is the devil's counterfeit for love. There is
nothing more beautiful on earth than a pure
love and there is nothing so blighting as lust.*
D. L. MOODY

❯ FOR FURTHER THOUGHT:

Do you view lust as a minor flaw or as a major sin?
How does your perspective match up with Jesus' own
words?

❯ PRACTICAL APPLICATION:

Are there any habits in your life—the movies you
watch, the places you go, the websites you visit—that
invite lust? If so, how can you start cutting out those
poisonous influences today?

---

*Almighty God, I know that You have the power
to help me escape lust—but I know I first have to
be willing. Conform my heart and mind to Your
standard. . .then give me the strength to run.*

GOSSIP—STOP IT!

A talebearer reveals secrets, but he who is
of a faithful spirit conceals the matter.
PROVERBS 11:13

Gossip is one of those all-too-common "little" sins. It's certainly not on par with the "biggies" like adultery, murder, or theft, right?

Well, if you read what the Bible has to say, you'll find that God takes gossip very, very seriously.

In the first chapter of Romans, Paul writes about God's punishment on sinful humans for their lawlessness. He goes on to provide a list of sinful individuals whose behavior makes them deserving of God's judgment. Right there in verse 29 is the word *whisperers* (which means "those who gossip").

Let's get real with ourselves here. God hates gossip, and He hates it because it destroys what He has created and has worked so hard to restore and protect—the name of another person.

So let's be very careful not just what we say *to* others but what we say *about* them. Let's think before we speak. Let's ask ourselves first if what we are about to say is true. Then let's ask ourselves if our words are loving and helpful. . .or if they just damage another's reputation.

And if the words we are about to speak don't pass muster, let's keep them to ourselves.

No surer sign of an unprofitable life than
when people give way to censoriousness and
inquisitiveness into the lives of other men.
FRANCIS DE SALES

⇢ FOR FURTHER THOUGHT:

When you have to offer criticism—to your kids,
a friend, or a coworker—do you stop at the negative
or end on a more positive note?

⇢ PRACTICAL APPLICATION:

The next time you open your mouth to say
something about a person, ask yourself whether
you'd like someone to say these words about *you*.

Lord God, the last thing I want to do is hurt someone
by tarnishing their name. Help me seek to build
up the integrity of others—not to tear it down.

DEPENDENCE IS GOOD

Jesus looked at them and said to them, "With men this is impossible, but with God all things are possible."
MATTHEW 19:26

The rich young ruler's conversation with Jesus had not gone as expected. Instead of learning that he had fulfilled all the requirements of the law—which he thought would admit him to heaven—the young man was told to sell his possessions and give to the poor. Dejected, he gave up and went home.

This turn of events prompted much discussion between Jesus and His disciples about the difficulties of being admitted to heaven. Frustrated with the impossible scenario Jesus was painting (complete with camels going through the eye of a needle), the disciples finally asked: "Who then can be saved?" (19:25).

In response, Jesus zeroed in on the heart of the matter: no one can be saved by their own efforts! The rich young ruler had tried everything humanly possible, and still he came up short. Man's greatest efforts pale in comparison to the requirements of a holy God.

But grace, freely offered by God and accepted by individuals, will admit us to heaven. God calls us to remember that with Him, all things *are* possible—even eternal life for the worst of sinners. Realizing we can do nothing is the key to gaining everything.

Your salvation does not depend on what
you are but on what He is. For every
look at self, take ten looks at Christ.
F. B. Meyer

⇥ FOR FURTHER THOUGHT:

Why do riches and fame often interfere with people's ability to trust God and depend on Him for salvation?

⇥ PRACTICAL APPLICATION:

How dependent on God would you say you are? How could you improve that score?

I know I can't save myself, God, so I'm
depending fully on You to do what I can't.
Teach me humility and reliance—that's the
only way I can live up to Your high calling.

OVERCOME EVIL WITH GOOD

And [David] said to his men, "The LORD
forbid that I should do this thing to my master,
the LORD's anointed, to stretch out my hand
against him, since he is the anointed of the LORD."
So David stopped his servants with these words
and did not allow them to rise against Saul.

1 SAMUEL 24:6–7

This was David's perfect opportunity to take out his powerful persecutor. As King Saul prowled through the wilderness in search of David, he ducked into a cave to use the restroom. Little did he know this cave was David's hiding place!

David's men, assuming that the Lord had arranged this opportunity, encouraged him to kill Saul. But David knew better and resisted the urge to sin.

"He not only would not do this bad thing himself, but he would not suffer those about him to do it," the old-time commentator Matthew Henry wrote. "Thus he rendered good for evil, to him from whom he received evil for good; and was herein an example to all who are called Christians, not to be overcome of evil, but to overcome evil with good."

These words echo apostle Paul's theme in Romans 12:21: "Do not be overcome by evil, but overcome evil with good."

As Christians, we all have opportunities to sin against our enemies. But God calls us to rise above our baser instincts. If we submit to His Spirit, who lives within, He'll provide all the strength we need to overcome evil with good.

Though justice be thy plea, consider this,
That, in the course of justice, none of us
should see salvation: we do pray for mercy.
WILLIAM SHAKESPEARE

❖ FOR FURTHER THOUGHT:

How do you think God feels when He judges sinners?

❖ PRACTICAL APPLICATION:

How might the answer to that question change how
you respond to the urge for retribution or revenge?

Lord, I never want to respond to my enemy's
hurtful actions and remarks by sinking to his
level. Teach me how to take the higher path
and answer any offense with kindness.

STAY FAITHFUL

"The Lord God is my strength, and He
will make my feet like deer's feet, and He
will make me walk on my high places."
Habakkuk 3:19

Today's scripture is the high point of Habakkuk's prophecy. Don't you love the imagery of God strengthening you to scale mountains like a surefooted deer?

But the images that precede this picture aren't as pleasant. God had condemned His people for violence, drunkenness, and idolatry, threatening them with punishment. Unable to argue with God's assessment, Habakkuk simply promised to stay faithful. "Although the fig tree shall not blossom, fruit shall not be on the vines, the labor of the olive shall fail, the fields shall yield no food, the flock shall be cut off from the fold, and there shall be no herd in the stalls, yet I will rejoice in the Lord. I will rejoice in the God of my salvation" (3:17–18).

Let's choose to be like Habakkuk. Whatever hardships we face, may we stay faithful and "rejoice in the Lord." Make the conscious choice to honor God first. *Then* you'll climb the mountains.

Do not pray for easy lives, pray to be stronger men.
PHILLIPS BROOKS

⇢ FOR FURTHER THOUGHT:

How faithful are you—not just to God but to others?

⇢ PRACTICAL APPLICATION:

If you make a promise—to your wife, kids, neighbor, or coworker—do everything within your power to keep that promise, even if it means making a hard sacrifice. Once you learn to be faithful to others, faithfulness to God will come more naturally.

---

*Heavenly Father, I've made up my mind—
I'm going to follow You no matter what.
Even in the midst of unthinkable tragedies,
help me follow through on this promise.*

IN THE LORD ALONE

*You will show me the path of life. In Your
presence is fullness of joy; at Your right
hand there are pleasures forevermore.*

PSALM 16:11

As you read the book of Psalms, you don't want to miss one
of its top themes: *Everything* you desire, want, and need is
found in the Lord alone. So why look anywhere else?

As seen in today's verse (and many others throughout
his psalms), David lived out this conviction. That's why,
when he once lost this vital focus, his heart wandered
and he broke half of the Ten Commandments in one fell
swoop. It's crucial that we grab on and hold tightly to this
core conviction.

Not surprisingly, David's fellow psalmists emphasized
this theme as well. In Psalm 73:25, for instance, Asaph
writes: "Whom have I in heaven but You? And there is none
on earth that I desire besides You." Powerful words, indeed.

Jesus said it best in Matthew 6:21, "For where your
treasure is, there your heart will be also." It's not enough
just to believe in God and His home in heaven. God calls
you to *want* Him. . .and Him alone.

*Sufficient grace is not just enough to survive,
but enough to have supernatural joy in the
midst of anything He allows us to go through.*
JAMES MACDONALD

❯❯ FOR FURTHER THOUGHT:

Are you trusting God as your ultimate satisfaction,
or are worldly things—even those that would
otherwise be harmless—starting to take His place?

❯❯ PRACTICAL APPLICATION:

How can you begin to view your true treasure as
heavenly, not as the things of this earth? Are there
any physical things you can actually give up for God?

---

*Thank You, God, for supplying all my
needs. Help me never to seek safety, joy,
or meaning in earthly pursuits, which can
never give me even one of these things.*

NOTHING COMPARES TO JESUS

*I count all things but loss for the excellency of
the knowledge of Christ Jesus my Lord.*
PHILIPPIANS 3:8

What does it mean to "know" Jesus? You might think it simply means acknowledging that a carpenter from Galilee named Jesus died on a cross and that God accepted His sacrifice as payment for humanity's sins. But is that all Jesus was? A good man? An enlightened teacher? An anointed miracle-worker?

No. Jesus was far, far more. Before time began, He shared incomparable glory with God His Father in heaven (John 17:5). He is the eternal Word who is *with* God and who *is* God—and who created everything in the entire universe (John 1:1–3). He is the express image of God in all His glory (Hebrews 1:3). When John saw Jesus in heaven in His full magnificence and power, he was overcome with awe and fell down at His feet as dead (Revelation 1:13–17).

To know Jesus is to know Him as God. If you could see Him for even a moment as Paul saw Him, you would agree that everything in this world is worth very little compared to the precious privilege of knowing the Lord.

Long for nothing, desire nothing, hope for nothing, but to have all that is within thee changed into the spirit and holy temper of the holy Jesus. Let this be thy Christianity, thy church, and thy religion.
WILLIAM LAW

❯❯ FOR FURTHER THOUGHT:

What does your faith mean to you? Is it a series of facts that you believe, or is it a mutual, ongoing relationship with Jesus that spills over into every aspect of your life?

❯❯ PRACTICAL APPLICATION:

The next time you study the Bible, think of how each truth you uncover points back to Jesus—and then search for ways in which it applies to your own spiritual walk.

Lord, it's sometimes easy to reduce the life-changing truths of Your Word down to mere trivia in my mind. Continuously remind me of Your glory so that I can live a life full of awe and wonder.

SO MUCH MORE

You have surrounded me behind and before and
laid Your hand on me. Such knowledge is too
wonderful for me; it is high; I cannot attain it.
PSALM 139:5–6

Christopher Columbus set out to blaze a new route to the West Indies. Instead of finding a new shipping route, this adventurer located a new continent. Even today, people celebrate his undertaking.

Learning more about God is its own adventure. You might have your own ideas about who He is—only to learn all of them are wrong or incomplete. You might think He's a God of justice only to discover His mercy and grace. You might think He's a God who holds grudges only to learn He's ready and willing to forgive. You might think God is your "cosmic buddy" only to discover He's holy and worthy of profound honor and respect.

God is good and kind, but He's also powerful and just. He cares about your deepest needs while holding the world together. He extends grace but asks for obedience. A journey with God is both the deepest blessing and the most challenging journey you'll ever know. God is more than you dreamed of when you first believed. The one who made, loves, and understands you also calls you to spend time getting to know Him.

Your adventure with God leads to daily discoveries. Expect surprises. Be grateful. Express joy. Live knowing God's mercy is new every morning for the rest of your life.

Our lives are a voyage of discovery.
JOHN STOTT

❖ FOR FURTHER THOUGHT:

Why do you think God has arranged our spiritual lives so that we discover Him slowly, not all at once?

❖ PRACTICAL APPLICATION:

Are you content to learn about God one step at a time? Have you stalled in your spiritual education, or are you continually moving forward?

Thank You, God, for allowing me to uncover tiny portions of Your mysteries. I want to keep learning until the day I see You face-to-face. . . and all my hardest questions are resolved at once.

BE CAREFUL WHAT
YOU LOOK AT

"I made a covenant with my eyes.
Why then should I think on a maid?"

Job 31:1

You probably know this already, but if you were to poll the guys at your weekly Bible study about their top struggle in the Christian walk, it would probably have something to do with sexual lust. They'd likely tell you that their eyes go where they shouldn't, and then it's only a matter of moments before the mind follows.

God calls us to avoid lust-inducing images. But in today's world, that's easier said than done. We live in an R-rated world. Even the PG-rated shows often, if not usually, include scenes that can cause the mind to wander into unholy waters. Not even sports programming or everyday advertising is safe.

So how do we win this battle? It's a matter of commitment—or, as Job put it, making a covenant with our eyes to not look at images that cause us to stumble.

Today, make a covenant with your eyes to not intentionally view lust-inducing images. And when you make a commitment to focus on the right things—namely, your love for your family and your God—you will find yourself winning the battle for your mind.

No one is immune to temptation. Not even a hero. Not even a nobody. Not even people like you and me. Lust is never very far away. And just when you least expect it, there it is again.
CHARLES SWINDOLL

» FOR FURTHER THOUGHT:

Make a list of the times you've fallen into lust recently. Then trace each of those instances back to their source.

» PRACTICAL APPLICATION:

With God's help, what are some steps you can take to avoid those sources in the future?

Lord, I never want to abuse Your sacrifice by wasting my time on unholy lusts. Give me the discernment and courage to combat these emotions and become more like You.

CALLED TO LOVE

*"But I say to you who hear: Love your enemies.
Do good to those who hate you. Bless those who
curse you, and pray for those who spitefully use you."*
LUKE 6:27–28

Have you ever thought of where humanity would be if God had looked down on sinful, lost people and just said, "Fine! They hate Me, they curse My name, and they live lives that offend Me in every way. I'm through with them!"

The Bible teaches that you were once God's enemy (Romans 5:10), alienated from and hostile toward Him (Colossians 1:21). But it also teaches that while you were still a sinner, Jesus, God's only Son, died for you so that you could be reconciled to Him (Romans 5:8).

God tells you to love your enemies, and He tells you to do good for those who hate you and curse you. But more than simply telling you to do those things, He *showed* you what that kind of love and blessing really looks like by sending Jesus to die on the cross.

It's not easy to love and bless people who don't reciprocate. But God calls you to do just that. Only then can you give those people a much-needed glimpse of what God's love is all about.

The God of Christianity never claims to be fair. He goes beyond fair. The Bible teaches that he decided not to give us what we deserve—that's mercy. In addition, God decided to give us exactly what we didn't deserve—we call that grace.
ANDY STANLEY

❯ FOR FURTHER THOUGHT:

When have you gone out of your way to bless someone who mistreated you?

❯ PRACTICAL APPLICATION:

How might remembering our own sin help us react appropriately when others mistreat us?

Lord Jesus, without Your grace, I know I'd have no chance for salvation. So teach me how to offer this grace toward others, even when I feel like grace is the last thing they deserve.

THE RULE OF 490

Then Peter came to Him and said, "Lord, how often shall my brother sin against me and I forgive him? Up to seven times?" Jesus said to him, "I do not say to you, up to seven times, but up to seventy times seven."

MATTHEW 18:21–22

How many times do you forgive someone before cutting them out of your life? According to Jewish law at the time of Jesus, you should forgive someone three times. That comes from Old Testament passages in Amos and Job, where God forgave nations who oppressed Israel three times before bringing judgment against them.

When Peter doubled the number and added one, he likely thought he was being generous. But Jesus took Peter's example to the extreme. We can easily remember if we've forgiven someone three or even seven times for some repeated offense, but to keep track of whether it's been 486 times or 499 times seems ludicrous. Essentially, Jesus was telling His disciples to stop keeping track. Their job (and ours) is to just keep forgiving from the heart.

God doesn't stop forgiving us at 490 times, or at 490,000. He just keeps forgiving us. And because we've been forgiven, we are called and able to forgive others like the Lord does—which is to say, every single time someone needs it.

*There is only one cure for the cancer of
bitterness. That is to forgive the perceived
offender once and for all, with God's help.*
JAMES DOBSON

❯❯ FOR FURTHER THOUGHT:

Why must forgiveness be open-ended? What would
happen if there were limits to forgiveness, either God's
or our own?

❯❯ PRACTICAL APPLICATION:

When you struggle with an unforgiving spirit, ask God
to remind you of His ongoing mercy in your life.

---

*Father, help me forgive like You do—not counting
the times I've been hurt by someone's sin, but
remembering the countless times You've forgiven me.*

MOVING PAST ARROGANCE

How long shall they utter and speak hard things,
and all the workers of iniquity boast in themselves?
PSALM 94:4

The Bible has its fair share of leading characters who let arrogance lead them to personal ruin. Moses killed a man, David committed adultery, and Paul sought to harm the very people Jesus came to rescue. Each man acted as if God's law didn't apply to him. They justified each decision based on their desired outcome.

Pride and false humility are two sides of the same coin. One side wants to be noticed and the other wants to be noticed by saying it doesn't want to be noticed. Both shine a light on self.

When Jesus points you toward true life, you should expect Him to do two things. The first is to teach you that who you are is all about who *He* is and what *He's* done. Nothing you can do changes who you are to God (see Ephesians 2:9). The second is that when you take credit for something God has done through you, it will be the only credit you receive (see Matthew 6:5).

Arrogance is the source of man's downfall because it replaces God's perfection with man's misguided intentions, resulting in self-worship. And nobody wants to see that. God called Moses, David, and Paul out of their arrogance and led them into a humble acceptance of the true source of their success. He can do the same for you.

*A lifetime of putting yourself at the center
of your own universe will turn you into a
caricature of low ideals and degrading habits.
It will sink you into the mire of competition,
trap you in a cycle of never-satisfied desires,
and steal from you the joys of simple serenity.*
CLAIRE AND CURT CLONINGER

✤ FOR FURTHER THOUGHT:

Whenever you express humility, are you trying to
follow God's laws, or are you merely *acting* humble,
hoping others will see how righteous you are?

✤ PRACTICAL APPLICATION:

If you find that your motivations for humility are misguided, admit it to God and ask Him to change your
attitude.

---

*I know I have no reason for pride, Father.
I can't do anything—let alone be a good
person—without Your help. Teach me to point
to You as the source of every good deed I do.*

SERVING OTHERS

*And He sat down and called the twelve and
said to them, "If any man desires to be first, the
same shall be last of all and servant of all."*

MARK 9:35

Many men are leery of the concept of servanthood. They
understand the need to love their fellow man, to live virtuous
lives, and to even occasionally go out of their way to lend a
hand—but the idea of being a servant to everyone? *That's
nonsense—it's just not practical!*

Yet Jesus stated this truth on more than one occasion.
In Mark's Gospel, He said, "If any man desires to be first,
the same shall be last of all and servant of all." This needs to
be understood in context. His disciples had been arguing
which of them would be greatest in Jesus' coming kingdom.
They all wanted to be first. Jesus, however, informed them
that if they *truly* wanted to be first, they must put themselves
last in their own lives.

The disciples' exalted position in heaven depended on
how badly they wanted it. If they served others, God would
see to it that they were rewarded beyond measure. But if
they didn't want to pay such a price, they'd still go to heaven;
they just wouldn't be as greatly rewarded there. There was
no compulsion. It was up to them.

Christ called them to "lay up for [themselves] treasures
in heaven" (Matthew 6:20), and then He told them a surefire
way to obtain that eternal reward. The question is this: How
badly do *you* want it?

*One can so easily become too great to be used by
God. One can never be too small for His service.*
CORRIE TEN BOOM

❧ FOR FURTHER THOUGHT:

If you appeared before God today, how pleased do you
think He'd be with your service toward others?

❧ PRACTICAL APPLICATION:

Look for opportunities to serve someone today—even
if that person is someone you don't know or aren't
comfortable speaking with.

---

*Lord, I don't want to do just the bare minimum
for You. Give me a servant's heart so that I can
show others how wonderful it is to be Your child.*

THE JOY OF DOING RIGHT

Blessed is the man who does not walk in the counsel of the ungodly or stand in the way of sinners or sit in the seat of the scornful.

PSALM 1:1

There is no joy greater than that of having done the right thing, even if those around you have not.

God knows what is in our hearts and minds. He loves us and cares about us so much that he takes an intimate interest in everything we do. May He never see us making bad decisions or following the mistakes of others!

Unfortunately, this is exactly what He does sees on occasion. Christianity is available to everyone—there's no lower or upper intelligence limit. But not everyone chooses to make smart decisions. Sometimes, it's so much easier to simply go along with the crowd. It temporarily takes the pressure off and makes us feel better. Later, however, we realize a horrible truth: we have pushed ourselves away from the Lord.

The next time you're tempted to follow the crowd, remember the very first verse of Psalms. What a joy it is to do the right thing!

The issue is not whether everybody else is doing it. The issue is whether it is right or wrong.
NATHANIEL AND HANS BLUEDORN

›› FOR FURTHER THOUGHT:

How committed are you to following God instead of the crowd?

›› PRACTICAL APPLICATION:

How can you keep your head above the shifting morality of your culture? Who is available to help you?

I know You've called me to follow You, God, but the voices of culture sometimes seem to drown out Your voice. Speak to me in the midst of this noise so that I can maintain my loyalty to You.

DO YOU WELCOME A REBUKE?

The king of Israel said to Jehoshaphat, "There is
still one man, Micaiah the son of Imlah, by whom
we may inquire of the LORD. But I hate him, for
he does not prophesy good concerning me, but evil."
And Jehoshaphat said, "Let the king not say so."
1 KINGS 22:8

It's human nature to only want good news, and the king of Israel routinely turned to people who said just what he wanted to hear. This was disastrous not only for him but for his family and all who depended on his leadership. By preferring his own wisdom, and by refusing to heed the warnings of God's true messengers, Ahab lost the position and power he'd valued so highly.

How do you respond to the rebuke of a friend or the warning of a trusted mentor? Are you willing to accept tough words and rethink your course, even if the thought of it makes you uncomfortable? God's warnings are rarely what we want to hear, but He still calls us to listen. In reality, it might be the very thing that saves you and your loved ones from ruin.

The sting of a reproach is the truth of it.
BENJAMIN FRANKLIN

✥ FOR FURTHER THOUGHT:

What would the world be like if "confirmation bias"—
the tendency to accept only what we want to hear—
didn't exist?

✥ PRACTICAL APPLICATION:

Do you have any such biases in your own life? If so,
what steps can you take to overcome them?

---

*Father, I don't want to behave like I have a
monopoly on truth. Open my eyes and ears to
the greater truths You're calling me to learn.*

BOLD ENOUGH TO ASK

And behold, two blind men sitting by the wayside,
when they heard that Jesus was passing by, cried out,
saying, "Have mercy on us, O Lord, Son of David."
MATTHEW 20:30

When life is good and problems are few, you might think you have less need for God. You might spiritualize your attitude by thinking you're relieving God of the burden of taking care of you. If you can meet your own needs, maybe God is simply an option for when things get tough.

Interestingly, the greater your need, the more likely you are to boldly make requests to God. All Christians have a moment in their faith journey when they discover it's impossible to manage life alone.

This was the case with two blind men who encountered Jesus. Having heard the stories of healing, restoration, and forgiveness, these men made their audacious request to Jesus and trusted enough to ask for mercy. Their bold faith was rewarded—they started by hearing His voice, and they ended up seeing His face.

Before you see God's plan, God calls you to believe. This was true for two blind men, and it's equally true in your personal journey with Jesus.

Come boldly into his throne of grace—even when you have sinned and failed. He forgives—instantly—those who repent with godly sorrow.
DAVID WILKERSON

» FOR FURTHER THOUGHT:

Why do you think God values confidence in our prayers?

» PRACTICAL APPLICATION:

Practice being bold with God. Whenever you have a need, no matter how improbable it may seem, define it simply and concisely in prayer. Then wait for His reply, trusting that He knows best.

Thank You, Almighty God, for giving me the privilege to come boldly before You whenever I want. Teach me how to make full use of this amazing opportunity each day.

SAVED TO SERVE

The righteous considers the cause of the poor,
but the wicked does not care to know it.

PROVERBS 29:7

At times within Christianity, certain teaching arises saying that faith should be defined by our acts of compassion. However well-intentioned this might be, the thinking is exactly backward—it places works of compassion ahead of the biblical teaching of salvation by faith alone.

The Bible consistently and explicitly teaches that salvation can't be earned—that it comes as a result of faith in the work of Jesus Christ on the cross. But scripture also teaches that true saving faith *will* result in a heart of compassion for those Jesus called "the least of these." That is what James meant when he wrote, "Faith, if it does not have works, is dead" (James 2:17).

Your concern for the plight of the needy won't save you, and neither will any amount of humanitarian or charity work. Rather, your concern for others serves as visible evidence that you are a true follower of Christ.

God calls you to trust Him for your own salvation. When you do, He will motivate you and empower you to serve others.

None can trust in the merits of Christ,
till he has utterly renounced his own.
JOHN WESLEY

❖ FOR FURTHER THOUGHT:

Why do you think God says it's impossible to earn
salvation on your own—even through noble deeds
such as serving others?

❖ PRACTICAL APPLICATION:

When you sense a need, pray before you act. Ask God
to ensure that your compassionate efforts are based on
His prior love for you, not an attempt to win His love.

Lord God, I know there's nothing I can do to
earn salvation or even Your approval. Help me
rely solely on Your grace. . .and then motivate
me to shine Your light to everyone I see.

A MOST IMPORTANT COMMAND

If a man says "I love God" and hates his brother,
he is a liar, for how can he who does not love his
brother, whom he has seen, love God, whom he has
not seen? And we have this commandment from
Him: that he who loves God also loves his brother.

1 John 4:20–21

Let's face it: some people are very difficult to love. They're too loud, too opinionated, too overbearing, too unlearned, too. . .well, you get the point. But the apostle John has some very strong words as to how we as followers of Christ are to relate to even the most unlovable among us.

If you can't love someone who's right in front of you, John taught, *then how can you say you love a God you can't even see?* The answer is simple: we can't. And if we say we can, John said we're liars.

Ouch!

So when you encounter one of the "unlovable" people (and there are plenty of them out there), approach them the way Jesus did—with unconditional, sacrificial love. And when your words and acts of love don't change a person in the least, love them all the more. It's God's job to change people—your job is simply to love them the same way He loves you.

*What's not so popularly understood is that the
cross was intended to work two ways: vertically,
to heal our irreconcilable differences with God,
and horizontally, to heal our irreconcilable
differences with each other. The cross must stand
between us and the heavenly Father, but the
cross also must stand between you and me.*
GARY KINNAMAN

❯ FOR FURTHER THOUGHT:

Why do you think God calls us to love everyone—
even the people who hate us?

❯ PRACTICAL APPLICATION:

How well are you living up to this command?
Ask God to empower you to do better.

---

*Loving Father, I need Your strength to overcome
my natural tendency to despise my enemies.
Teach me how to rise above the waters of hate
so that I can truly love the unlovable.*

OUTWARD APPEARANCES

But the LORD said to Samuel, "Do not look at his appearance or at the height of his stature, because I have refused him. For the LORD does not see as man sees. For man looks at the outward appearance, but the LORD looks at the heart."

1 SAMUEL 16:7

You probably don't need to reread today's scripture to know that people with an appealing physical appearance (men and women alike) have many advantages in life. It's just part of fallen human nature to equate "the look" with important character traits that have nothing to do with appearance.

But God doesn't care what men look like or how tall they are or what they've accomplished in this life. He concerns Himself only with what is in their heart and mind.

Even more, He calls us to adopt His better standard. We should make sure we never judge or evaluate anyone, including ourselves, based on physical appearance. And we should evaluate our own hearts to make sure we are focused on pleasing God in every area of our lives.

It's not a natural attitude, but it is supernatural. God is happy to help us obey His command when we ask.

External beauty cannot hide internal ugliness.
Neil Anderson and Dave Park

❖ FOR FURTHER THOUGHT:

How much of the hatred and bitterness in today's culture do you think stems solely from the unwillingness to look beyond a person's exterior?

❖ PRACTICAL APPLICATION:

Make a habit of questioning first impressions. The next time you meet someone, pay attention to the subconscious assumptions your brain makes about that person's character based on appearances. Then try finding evidence to contradict these assumptions.

Lord, I know that many of the godliest men and women in history were plain and unassuming. Give me the wisdom and discernment to see past the surface and into the heart.

GOD HONORS HARD WORK

The soul of the sluggard desires and has nothing,
but the soul of the diligent shall be made prosperous.
PROVERBS 13:4

It might be hard to believe, especially on Monday morning, but from the very beginning, God intended man to work. His first assignment for Adam was to live in the garden of Eden and "to dress it and to take care of it" (Genesis 2:15). Sadly, when Adam and Eve sinned, work turned into toil—and it's stayed that way ever since (see Genesis 3).

But the fact remains: God calls you to work and produce. In today's scripture, He warns against laziness and encourages us to pursue hard, diligent work. God says that laziness leads to poverty. . .and that the diligent will find their needs are met.

So work hard. Approach your day job with commitment and passion. And as you work to provide for yourself and your family, don't forget Paul's words: "Therefore, whether you eat or drink, or whatever you do, do all for the glory of God" (1 Corinthians 10:31).

When the precepts and example of Jesus Christ fully interpermeate society, to labor with the hands will be regarded not only as a duty but a privilege.
CATHERINE BEECHER

❖ FOR FURTHER THOUGHT:

How eager are you to work? Do you approach each day with an attitude of "I *have* to do this" or an attitude of "I *get* to do this"?

❖ PRACTICAL APPLICATION:

Memorize Bible verses that speak of the importance of work. Then if you show up for work with a negative attitude, quote these verses to yourself throughout the day.

Thank You, God, for giving me the ability to work. I never want to take such a privilege for granted—teach me how to rejoice in my labor.

SLOW, STEADY PROGRESS

The end of a thing is better than its beginning.
And the patient in spirit is better
than the proud in spirit.
ECCLESIASTES 7:8

If you've ever been to a rally—spiritual, sports, political, or business-related—then you know how a great message can fire up a crowd. Everybody's eager to go home and implement what they learned, but as soon as you walk through the door, reality strikes.

The sink is backed up, the car needs repairs, someone needs a ride to soccer practice, and the baby is crying. So we dive into these responsibilities, and our enthusiasm fades as quickly as it came. We're like the man "who hears the word and immediately receives it with joy. Yet he has no root in himself, but endures for a while" (Matthew 13:20–21).

In today's scripture, God calls us to be patient as we set our minds on something. If your goal is to read God's Word every day but your responsibilities are getting in the way, try getting up a little earlier. If your goal is to walk five miles a day, start with one mile and work your way up. If your goal is to set a new sales record, study the current leader and carefully implement his strategies.

Slow, steady progress beats quick, emotional commitment every time. The end is better than the beginning.

Determination fades quickly without endurance.
STEVE CAMPBELL

❖ FOR FURTHER THOUGHT:

What percentage of tasks that you set out to complete actually get completed?

❖ PRACTICAL APPLICATION:

What steps can you take to boost your endurance? What role do God, scripture, friends, and family play in your progress?

God, I don't want to live a life full of loose ends and good intentions. Give me the endurance I need to stick with every task—big or small—to the very end.

REDEEMING THE PAST

"And I will restore to you the years that the locust has eaten, the cankerworm, and the caterpillar, and the palmerworm, My great army that I sent among you."

JOEL 2:25

Regret is a terrible feeling for any man, including men of God. Regret causes you to look back at your mistakes, indiscretions, and missed opportunities and think, *If I could only go back to that time in my life, I'd do so much differently.*

Nearly every man has things in his past he's not proud of—things he knows God would not approve of if he did them now. But God promises to redeem your mistakes, sins, and missteps and use them for His glory and your good.

That is partly what the apostle Paul meant when he wrote, "We know that *all* things work together for good for those who love God, for those who are called according to His purpose" (Romans 8:28, emphasis added).

The past is just that—the past. There's nothing you can do to change it. You can't undo the things you wish you hadn't done, and you can't redo the things you wish you had. But God calls you to bring your past to Him. When you do, He'll find a way to redeem even your worst mistakes and use them to build something good.

*As long as you are carrying a secret, as long as you are
trying to ease your conscience by telling God how sorry
you are, you are setting yourself up to repeat the past.*
ANDY STANLEY

⟩ FOR FURTHER THOUGHT:

In the Christian life, when does regret over a sin cross
the line from godly sorrow into unhealthy obsession?

⟩ PRACTICAL APPLICATION:

Have you ever felt overwhelmed with guilt? Do you
feel that way now? How might you use passages of
scripture to help you move on?

---

*Father, I know that even when I wasn't serving
You, You were using each of my choices—even
my mistakes—to bring me into Your kingdom.
Thank You for Your incomprehensible mercy.*

A PRIVILEGE AND RESPONSIBILITY

"Moreover, as for me, God forbid that I should sin against the LORD in ceasing to pray for you. But I will teach you the good and right way."

1 SAMUEL 12:23

The words of the prophet Samuel above are an important challenge to all Christian men to pray regularly about all things. . .and especially for one another.

Samuel was addressing his own people who had sinned terribly against God, even turning against Him by demanding a king to rule over them. Yet Samuel assured them that God had not rejected them, and he challenged them to serve the Lord and not turn away into idolatry (1 Samuel 12:20–22). Then Samuel promised that he would pray for the people, for to do otherwise would be a sin against God.

God calls you to come to Him in prayer. Prayer is a wonderful privilege, but it's also a responsibility. He wants you to bring Him requests for yourself, your family, your Christian brothers and sisters, for those who need Jesus, and for anyone or anything else He lays on your heart.

When your heart feels burdened over an issue or situation, talk it over with God—He *wants* to hear from you.

*Seek the welfare of others. Find out how you can be
a blessing. Pray for the city you live in right now
and its people, for its welfare and your welfare.
This is one of the fundamental keys. As you become
a blessing, you set yourself up to be blessed.*
TONY EVANS

❖ FOR FURTHER THOUGHT:

How closely do you listen to your coworkers, friends at
church, and family when they mention their needs or
concerns?

❖ PRACTICAL APPLICATION:

Write down each need you hear about—then pray for
that need as fervently as if it were your own.

---

*Father, I don't want to sin against You
by ceasing to pray for those around me.
Teach me to be more attentive to their
needs so that I can bring them to You.*

IN EVERY AREA OF LIFE

"But they did not listen or incline their ear,
but walked in the counsels and in the plans of their
evil hearts, and went backward and not forward."

JEREMIAH 7:24

Jews of Jeremiah's time excelled at following the external trappings of the law; as long as they offered the appropriate sacrifices in abundance, they thought they would please God.

But in Jeremiah 7:22–23, the Lord told them otherwise: "I did not speak to your fathers or command them concerning burnt offerings or sacrifices. But this thing I commanded them, saying. . .'Walk in *all* the ways that I have commanded you'" (emphasis added). But the people did as they wanted, resulting in a backward religion.

The literal wording of the last sentence of today's verse reads: "They *were* backward and not forward." They had their religion the wrong way around; they had focused on external actions and not internal obedience.

Earlier, the prophet Isaiah said that because the people had a "little" religion, they would fall backward into captivity: "The word of the LORD to them was 'Precept on precept, precept on precept, line on line, line on line, here a little and there a little,' that they might go and fall backward and be broken and snared and taken" (28:13).

The goal for Christians today remains the same: "This is the love of God, that we keep His commandments" (1 John 5:3). True devotion will express itself in every area of our lives.

God is impressed, not with noise or size or wealth,
but with quiet things. . .things done in secret—
the inner motives, the true heart condition.
CHARLES SWINDOLL

❯❯ FOR FURTHER THOUGHT:

How much of today's Christianity do you think is
sincere? How much of your own?

❯❯ PRACTICAL APPLICATION:

Are there any important areas in your walk with God
that you treat superficially? If so, how might you start
"getting serious" about those issues today?

It's easy, God, to treat Christianity like a comfortable,
cost-free routine. But I know Your calling is so
much greater than that. Teach me how to truly
obey You, no matter what I have to sacrifice.

CHECKLIST RELIGION

*"Good Master, what good thing shall I
do that I may have eternal life?"*
MATTHEW 19:16

A rich man met Jesus. He consulted his mental checklist and compared his past actions with what Jesus said he needed to do.

Don't murder? *Check.* Don't commit adultery? *Check.* Don't steal? *Check.* Don't lie? *Check.* Honor your parents? *Check.* Love your neighbor? *Check.* The rich man, feeling pretty good so far about his spiritual résumé, quickly said, "All these things I have kept from my youth. What do I still lack?" (verse 20).

Jesus said, "Go and sell what you have and give to the poor, and you shall have treasure in heaven. And come and follow Me" (verse 21). In this final to-do list, Jesus offered trust and friendship. This trust meant believing that God is worthy of greater faith than money. And the friendship invited the man to stay close and follow.

This is a beautiful picture of the new covenant that Jesus ushered in. What was once a checklist religion was transformed into a trusting friendship with God. God calls you to more than just a wall filled with impressive spiritual merit badges—He calls you to a deep, personal relationship. To settle for anything less is to trust your own efforts while resisting His help.

Christ is concerned with more than what we do. He is initially concerned about why we do what we do. Christ wants our external activities to be produced out of a personal relationship with Him. He demands something deeper than habit, more significant than ritual, more delightful than duty for duty's sake.

JOSEPH STOWELL

❖ FOR FURTHER THOUGHT:

How healthy is your relationship with God? Do you regularly commune with Him, or do your spiritual activities stop at the laws you obey?

❖ PRACTICAL APPLICATION:

What are some ways you can grow closer to God? When will you start?

Father, I never want my walk with You to degenerate into a mere list of dos and don'ts. Teach me how to live up to Your higher calling and seek a deeper relationship with You.

CALLED TO FOLLOW

Remember those who rule over you, who have
spoken to you the word of God. Follow their
faith, considering the result of their conduct.
HEBREWS 13:7

Western society puts great emphasis on being an independent, self-made man—being one's own boss. And while it's true that you must be able to stand on your own two feet and make your way in this world, there's also tremendous value in recognizing the authority of pastors and spiritual leaders. There's great wisdom in seeking the counsel of senior saints who have walked with God for many years and have much to teach. Consider "the result of their conduct"—the good fruit of a sincere Christian lifestyle and the wisdom that comes with years of serving the Lord and studying His Word.

It's no shame to admit you don't have all the answers. Submitting to spiritual leadership isn't a sign of weakness. Some men are afraid to let others teach them how to live. They think following others' instructions means checking their brain at the door. But that's not the case. Paul said, "Let us, therefore, as many as are perfect, be thus minded, and if in anything you are otherwise minded, God shall reveal even this to you" (Philippians 3:15).

So don't be afraid to follow the counsel of spiritual leaders and emulate the lifestyle of godly mentors. It's wise to seek out good role models. . .it's wise to be teachable.

*An occupational hazard of men is to
ignore experience and refuse to consult
others, especially those older than us.*
JEFFREY MILLER

❖ FOR FURTHER THOUGHT:

Why are men often seen as less willing to follow
instructions or seek advice?

❖ PRACTICAL APPLICATION:

How might the answer to the question above help you
understand the root of your own pride. . .as well as
how to improve?

---

*Thank You, Lord, for older Christians. I know each
one has great advice to offer and captivating stories to
tell—help me be humble enough to learn from them.*

"I'LL PRAY FOR YOU"

"My friends scorn me. But my eye pours out tears to God. O that one might plead for a man with God, as a man pleads for his neighbor!"

JOB 16:20–21

The Bible has a lot to teach us about how to pray, when to pray, and what to pray for. One type of prayer the Word tells us to engage in regularly is *intercession*, in which we "stand in the gap" before God on behalf of another person.

But just how important is this kind of prayer to God? So important that Jesus, His very own Son, is spending His time in heaven interceding for us this very moment (see Hebrews 7:23–28).

When a friend, family member, or fellow Christian is hurting and in need of a touch from God's hand, it's always good to offer comfort by promising to pray for that person. But as you spend time with the Lord, be sure to make good on that promise! God loves to answer His people's prayers, especially those prayers that stem from loving concern.

God calls you to make intercession for others a regular part of your prayer life. Someone may very well be counting on you.

*Intercessory prayer is an extension of the ministry
of Jesus through His body, the church, whereby
we mediate between God and humanity for
the purpose of reconciling the world to Him,
or between Satan and humanity for the
purpose of enforcing the victory of Calvary.*
DUTCH SHEETS

❯ FOR FURTHER THOUGHT:

What percentage of your prayers would you say are
intercessions for others?

❯ PRACTICAL APPLICATION:

Throughout your day, find ways to intercede. If a
coworker is having family issues, lift him up in prayer.
If a neighbor doesn't know Jesus, ask God to save his
soul. If your wife or kids are sick, ask God for healing.

*Thank You, Jesus, for interceding for me. I want to
show this act of kindness and grace to everyone You've
placed in my life. Reveal to me how I can begin today.*

PUT ON MERCY

For he who has shown no mercy shall have judgment
without mercy; and mercy rejoices over judgment.
JAMES 2:13

Be harsh with other people, and you can expect a substantial return on your investment. Mercy gives birth to mercy. . .and justice to justice. God offers you mercy and forgiveness, and He calls you to make this your go-to response toward others. Colossians 3:12–13 says, "Put on, therefore, as the elect of God, holy and beloved, hearts of mercies, kindness, humbleness of mind, meekness, long-suffering, being patient with one another and forgiving one another if any man has a quarrel against any. Even as Christ forgave you, so you also do."

God blesses those who show mercy (Matthew 5:7). In fact, He wants mercy even more than sacrifice (Matthew 9:13). An understanding of mercy can help you draw close to God (Hebrews 4:16). You don't have the right or even the ability to excuse sin in your own life, but you can meet other people in "Mercy Place" just beyond "Justice Junction."

Justice is the easy route right now, but it isn't God's route. His route is mercy, which takes the extra steps when the offender can't. His greatest priority is restoring relationships.

God calls you to let mercy rejoice over judgment.

Mercy begins with remembering our own deeds.
JAMES LUCAS

❯ FOR FURTHER THOUGHT:

When someone makes a mistake—intentional or not—do you try to see life from that person's point of view, or are you quick to jump to negative conclusions?

❯ PRACTICAL APPLICATION:

What steps can you take to fill up your "mercy meter"?

Lord Jesus, who am I to judge others for what they did to me when it was my sin that nailed You to the cross? Teach me how to forgive like You do.

KEEP A CLEAR CONSCIENCE

. . .holding faith and a good conscience,
which some having put away concerning
faith have made shipwreck.

1 TIMOTHY 1:19

John 3:36 says, "He who believes in the Son has everlasting life," so you clearly need faith in Jesus. But if you lack love for God and your fellow man and don't have a clear conscience, your faith won't be very strong.

If you willfully disobey God then refuse to repent and accept His forgiveness, you violate your conscience. You won't necessarily lose your connection with Christ, but you'll likely live in defeat and condemnation, not enjoying the freedom and assurance that's rightfully yours.

If you've sinned, repent, trusting that God will forgive you. How can you know He will do that? His Word promises: "If we confess our sins, He is faithful and just to forgive us our sins and to cleanse us from all unrighteousness" (1 John 1:9). "He who covers his sins shall not prosper, but whoever confesses and forsakes them shall have mercy" (Proverbs 28:13).

God longs to forgive you and set you free. He's calling you to live an overcoming, victorious life by His Spirit.

Conscience is God present in man.
VICTOR HUGO

❯ FOR FURTHER THOUGHT:

Are you careful to follow your conscience, or do you frequently disregard it? How did you respond the last time your conscience spoke?

❯ PRACTICAL APPLICATION:

How can you train yourself to slow down and listen to God's "still, small voice" inside?

---

*Thank You, Father, for the gift of Your Holy
Spirit, who guides me in the right direction.
Help me always be attentive to His leading—
I don't want to ignore the one who sanctifies me.*

CONQUERORS FORGIVE

If your enemy is hungry, give him bread to
eat, and if he is thirsty, give him water to
drink. For you shall heap coals of fire on his
head, and the LORD shall reward you.
PROVERBS 25:21–22

This verse defies human nature. The world's way is to bless one's friends and curse one's enemies. Forgiveness and mercy are foreign concepts. However, God's thoughts and ways are higher than man's (Isaiah 55:8), and this passage instructs Christians to provide their enemies with subsistence and care.

God calls believers to resist carnal thinking and embrace the central message of the cross: "Love your enemies. . .and pray for those who despitefully use you and persecute you" (Matthew 5:44). The end result of our humanitarianism is that we will heap burning coals on our enemy's head.

In Bible times, burning coals were placed below and above metals in a furnace. Consequently, the metal was liquefied and the dross fell to the bottom. So today's verse isn't a call to some backhanded benevolence intended to impose affliction on our enemies; it's a promise that loving such people will either melt them into repentance and lead them to God or aggravate their condemnation, making their malice even more inexcusable.

Those who seek revenge are the *conquered*, but those who forgive are *conquerors*.

Pour honey into hearts instead of vinegar.
AMY NAPPA

❯ FOR FURTHER THOUGHT:

Why is Jesus the ultimate example of repaying evil with good?

❯ PRACTICAL APPLICATION:

In what ways can you apply today's verse to your everyday life?

Lord God, the world is full of hate and vitriol as it is—I don't want to contribute any more to that poisonous cycle. Show me the better path. Teach me how to fight with weapons of kindness.

PRESUMPTUOUS SINS

Keep back Your servant also from presumptuous sins; let them not have dominion over me. Then I shall be upright, and I shall be innocent of the great transgression.
PSALM 19:13

In today's scripture, David asked God to keep him from presumptuous sins—that is, deliberate, intentional sins. He knew that when he willfully indulged in disobedient acts, they'd end up becoming habits that ruled over him. That's not to say unintentional sins cause any less harm than intentional ones—they just don't flow as readily from a person's heart and mind.

The last thing David wanted was to be guilty of "the great transgression," which some believe meant pride or even apostasy.

David knew his wicked heart well. He was a murderer and adulterer, and he lied to cover up both. He might have even been slothful, given that he chose to stay behind in Jerusalem when it was time for kings to go out to battle (2 Samuel 11:1). That's when he spiraled out of control.

How about you? How well do you know your own heart? What sort of gross, presumptuous sins is it capable of? Do you fear being guilty of the great transgression? God calls you to take David's prayer in today's verse and make it your own. Ask God to intervene, to rule your heart, and to keep you from stumbling.

*Most of us don't really know the deep thoughts
and intentions of our own hearts; therefore
we must rely upon the Spirit of God to try,
to prove and to reveal that which is within us.*
JANE HAMON

❯❯ FOR FURTHER THOUGHT:

Have you ever asked God for a "heart check-up"?
What did that examination reveal?

❯❯ PRACTICAL APPLICATION:

When your car breaks down or your kids misbehave
or you're presented with the opportunity to fudge
the truth, write down your response. A great way of
judging your heart's attitude is to observe your own
reactions to these small, everyday situations.

---

*Lord, please keep my heart pure and directed
solely toward You. If there's any vein of greed
or anger or selfishness in it, reveal it to me and
help me stamp it out before it starts to grow.*

HOW TO SUCCEED
IN THE LORD'S EYES

*Thus Solomon finished the house of the LORD and
the king's house, and he prosperously completed
all that came into his heart to make in the
house of the LORD and in his own house. And
the LORD appeared to Solomon by night.*

<small>2 CHRONICLES 7:11–12</small>

When a man of God serves the Lord with fervor and zeal then later walks away from the Christian faith, it hurts. It hurts dozens, even hundreds, directly. It hurts thousands indirectly—for years to come. The damage is incalculable.

In biblical history, only a small number of men ever talked directly with the Lord. Yet King Solomon did twice. And not just for a brief moment or two. Solomon heard from God loud and clear. So, the first time you read the Bible, you have every reason to expect that Solomon is God's man through and through.

Then again, the Lord clearly warned Solomon two times that he wasn't exempt from becoming an absolute failure and an utter fool.

If Solomon was wholeheartedly devoted to God early on, he clearly became halfhearted as the years rolled on. Later in life, he became *no*-hearted. The one who could have taught the world about the Lord instead blatantly blasphemed His name. Scripture includes his story as a warning to us. Let's be sure we heed it.

*To espouse the truth, and then to fall
away, brings an ill report upon the gospel,
which will not go unpunished.*
THOMAS WATSON

✦ FOR FURTHER THOUGHT:

How does your spiritual life right now compare with
what it was when you first started your walk with God?
Is it stronger? The same? Weaker?

✦ PRACTICAL APPLICATION:

What steps can you take to ensure you're always
moving forward in your walk with God?

---

*Father, just like in an ordinary race, I sometimes
slow down in my Christian life. But I know
You've called me to keep running, so give
me the second wind I need to press on.*

DEFEATING THE DEVIL

But the Lord is faithful, who shall
establish you and keep you from evil.
2 THESSALONIANS 3:3

There will be times when you're under intense attack by the devil. Why then and not some other time? Probably because the devil—like a shark drawn by blood—senses when you're weak and most susceptible to temptation. Luke 4:13 says that after tempting Jesus, "he departed from Him for a season." Satan wasn't getting anywhere, so he retreated and waited for a future opportunity.

The Lord will not only empower you to withstand the enemy but protect you from his protracted attacks. But why would God allow a lengthy battle in the first place instead of just disposing of the devil? The answer is simple: to toughen you and demonstrate your resolve. You may not understand why God permits it, but you must trust Him just the same.

One of the Bible's most oft-quoted promises states, "Resist the devil and he will flee from you" (James 4:7). But he won't necessarily flee right away. Often, you'll be required to take a stand, defend your ground, and continue resisting. Finally, when Satan can't stand it anymore, he'll have no other option but to run.

"Oh," said the devil to Martin Luther, "you are a sinner." "Yes," said he, "Christ died to save sinners." Thus he smote him with his own sword.
CHARLES SPURGEON

❯ FOR FURTHER THOUGHT:

Sometimes, Christians think of Satan as merely an abstract, metaphorical being that symbolizes evil. What dangers are there in such thinking?

❯ PRACTICAL APPLICATION:

What forms of resistance can you practice against Satan's temptations? What can you learn from Jesus' example in Luke 4?

God, I know You've called me to a life of perpetual warfare against evil, but I could never do it without the tools You provide. Thank you for empowering me to fight the devil's schemes.

CHOOSE LIFE

"The thief does not come except to steal and to kill and to destroy. I have come that they might have life, and that they might have it more abundantly."
JOHN 10:10

Too often, the negatives of life seem to outweigh the positives. The bills are piling up. Your friends and family need your time and attention. So does your boss. You're exhausted and mentally drained. Life begins to cave in around you. It's just too much!

God's Word, though, exposes the lie (and the liar) behind these defeating thoughts. We have an enemy who rejoices when we believe such negative things. He wants only destruction for our souls. But Jesus calls us to a better, more victorious life. We only have to choose it—an act of the will blended with faith.

God is always a gentleman—He's not going to force His life on us. But when we rely on Him alone, He'll enable us to not only survive but thrive in our daily routine.

Each day, let's decide to take hold of what Christ offers us—life to the fullest.

*We are committing an unspeakable
crime against ourselves when we drown
ourselves in negative thinking.*
Maxie Dunnam

❯ FOR FURTHER THOUGHT:

Why is it so easy to default to negative thinking?
What are the dangers of negativity?

❯ PRACTICAL APPLICATION:

In every seemingly negative situation, force yourself to
make a list—physical or mental—of the reasons why
things aren't as bad as they appear.

---

*Life can get rough at times, Lord, but thanks to Your
grace, I don't have to let it get to me. Help me always
see the bright side, even when life is at its darkest.*

TRAIN HARD

*Beloved, when I gave all diligence to write to
you of the common salvation, it was necessary
for me to write to you and exhort you that
you should earnestly contend for the faith
that was once delivered to the saints.*
JUDE 3

The Greek word rendered "earnestly contend," according
to Bible commentator Albert Barnes, is a reference to the
ancient Grecian games. In other words, Jude was asking his
readers to put the same amount of effort into proclaiming
the gospel as Olympic athletes put into their games.

The athlete trains his body through daily rituals. He
gets up early, works hard for several hours, eats the right
foods, hydrates properly, gets ample rest, and then does the
same thing every day for years on end. . .all in preparation
for one event.

This is the type of dedication to the gospel that Jude is
calling us all to demonstrate. Training for the Olympics can
never be lackluster—and neither can our training to repre-
sent the gospel either. God may be calling you to contend
for the faith today. Have you put in the necessary training?

Responding to God's discipline brings immediate benefits. When we allow discipline to train us, we not only escape our sin, but we also grow in maturity.
Bruce Wilkinson

❯❯ FOR FURTHER THOUGHT:

What are some ways you have trained to stand up for the gospel? Scripture memorization? Prayer time? Humble service for others?

❯❯ PRACTICAL APPLICATION:

What other "spiritual exercises" can you add to your daily routine?

Father, I don't want to neglect my spiritual training, even when it feels too tiring or burdensome. Give me the patience and consistency to train each day.

INCONVENIENT EMERGENCIES

"You shall not see your brother's donkey or his ox fall down by the way and hide yourself from them. You shall surely help him to lift them up."
DEUTERONOMY 22:4

Helping others takes time. But the problem is that when we see someone who needs help, we're often on our way to work or heading to an appointment and can't afford to be late. In such cases, we must help anyway, trusting God that He'll take care of the consequences.

God also said, "If you see the donkey of him who hates you lying under its burden and would refrain from helping it, you shall surely help with it" (Exodus 23:5). Help your *enemy* when he has car problems? Isn't God judging him? Shouldn't you smile as you pass by and let him stew in his own juice?

No, God says—help him. You really have to trust the Lord on this, especially when your sense of vindictiveness is crying out for you to turn a blind eye. You have to overcome your selfish nature, which takes a conscious openness to God's leading.

Next time you come across an inconvenient emergency, stop, roll up your sleeves, and help that person in a hard situation.

Helping others means our ears and our eyes are open.
H. NORMAN WRIGHT

❯ FOR FURTHER THOUGHT:

When have you gone out of your way to help another person? Are you on the lookout for such opportunities each day?

❯ PRACTICAL APPLICATION:

Practice helping others by starting small. If your wife is cleaning the dishes, step in and finish for her. If your neighbor is mowing the lawn, offer to join in. Over time, the act of helping others will transform from a conscious effort into a natural response.

Thank You, Father, for the ways in which You help me each day, even when I don't deserve it. Grant me the opportunity today to do the same for somebody else.

SHAMELESS PERSISTENCE

"I say to you, though he will not rise and give to him because he is his friend, yet because of his persistence he will rise and give him as many as he needs."

LUKE 11:8

Jesus told a story about a man whose friend arrived at his house at midnight. The friend was famished, but the man had nothing to feed him. Then he realized that his neighbor probably had some bread. So he ran to his neighbor's house, beat on his door, and shouted till he woke him up. His neighbor crossly replied that the door was locked and he was in bed, so he wasn't about to get up and give him anything. The fact that they were friends made no difference.

But Jesus pointed out that if the man refused to take no for an answer and continued pounding and calling—shameless audacity at its finest—the neighbor *would* finally get up and give him bread. Jesus then applied this lesson to prayer: "And I say to you, ask, and it shall be given to you" (verse 9).

Now, don't miss the point: God isn't a grumpy neighbor! Rather, Jesus was emphasizing the importance of persistence. Sometimes, God calls you to state your request and state it again—and again and again, until the answer comes. Some people think that repeating a request shows a lack of faith, but Jesus Himself said otherwise.

So be shamelessly persistent.

He prays not at all, who does not press his plea.
E. M. BOUNDS

◈ FOR FURTHER THOUGHT:

Do you ever feel like you're annoying God with your prayers? What does the Bible say about that?

◈ PRACTICAL APPLICATION:

How can you commit to shameless, persistent prayer? Would a prayer journal, or an electronic app of some sort help?

---

*Lord God, I thank You for the assurance that
You're never annoyed by my repeated prayers.
I never want to tire of the act of praying.*

ENCOURAGING WORDS

Let no corrupt communication proceed out of your
mouth, but what is good for the use of edifying,
that it may minister grace to the hearers.
Ephesians 4:29

"Sticks and stones may break my bones, but words will never hurt me." This old saying just isn't true, however. Words can—and do—hurt. Ask anyone who was bullied as a child. Discouraging, shaming words can stay with a person for years, even decades.

As we spend less time talking and more time texting and giving status updates, let's also be aware that whatever we say online stays online. Sure, we can delete things, but others may have captured screenshots or printed our words. That Facebook rant about a friend or political party? It's out there. That post belittling a coworker? It's out there. That nasty, angry comment on a blog? It's out there.

As Ephesians 4:29 says, the words we choose are important. . .especially as the world becomes increasingly uninterested in the things of God. The way we talk, both online and off, can either attract people to Jesus or turn them away. Today, think about the language and tone you use while speaking. Are your word choices helpful? Are your phrases kind? Is your tone sarcastic? Cynical? Bitter? Ask God to help you think before you speak (or post!).

Because words have the power to affect people deeply, it is appropriate to consider how to encourage fellow Christians through what we say. Words can encourage, discourage, or do nothing.
LARRY CRABB

❖ FOR FURTHER THOUGHT:

Have you ever been hurt by someone's words? Have you ever spoken similar words to someone else?

❖ PRACTICAL APPLICATION:

If you've spoken hurtful words to someone, go and apologize to that person today—you never know how much that person might still be hurting.

Lord, I know You've called me to build others up with my words. . .but sometimes I'm tempted to tear them down. Sweeten my tongue with Your love and give me words that are pleasing to You.

CALLED TO BOLDNESS

"From now on the children of Israel must not come near the tabernacle of the congregation, lest they bear sin and die. But the Levites shall do the service of the tabernacle of the congregation, and they shall bear their iniquity. It shall be a statute forever throughout your generations."

NUMBERS 18:22–23

Imagine being told that you could not enter a sanctuary for worship ever again—that from that point on, only pastors and ministers were allowed in. After getting over the shock, you might start realizing the extent of God's holiness. Before Jesus took on flesh and dwelt among humanity, God could only be approached by the priests.

But praise God, Jesus made it possible for us to "come boldly to the throne of grace, that we may obtain mercy and find grace to help in time of need" (Hebrews 4:16).

After you've sinned, do you shy away from God, embracing an old covenant mindset? Or do you boldly approach the throne to receive mercy and help when you need it most?

*Without him, we are combustible matter
before a consuming fire, and cannot approach
to the throne of God with any success.*
STEPHEN CHARNOCK

» FOR FURTHER THOUGHT:

God no longer dwells in a temple; instead, He lives in
the hearts of each of His children. What does this say
about the effectiveness of Jesus' sacrifice in making us
holy?

» PRACTICAL APPLICATION:

Do you think of God as far away or unreachable, or do
you speak to Him like you would a close friend?

---

*Thank You, Jesus, for enabling me to experience
God first-hand instead of having to just take a
priest's word for it. Help me take advantage of
this wonderful opportunity every chance I get.*

MEANT FOR MORE

And let ours also learn to maintain good works
for necessary uses, that they are not unfruitful.
TITUS 3:14

The life of a Christ-follower is identified by action. Christians demonstrate love to others by being generous. They demonstrate they're trustworthy when they provide for their families. They do the hard things because they know the work they do is for God.

Today's verse isn't a promotion of self-reliance—you still need to depend on God for everything. But God has given you a job to help you be productive. Your salary helps provide for your family—and others whom you choose to help.

God has a plan for your life, and you can show your trust in that plan by taking the necessary action to finish well. Whatever plan He has for your life will also impact others. Money never advances God's objectives when it takes up permanent residence in your bank account. Use it wisely to bless others as well.

People who want to live generously are also servants—no more, no less—acting on behalf of a returning Prince. Wealth, resources, influence: these belong to the Prince. We must never forget this. And we put them to use in His name, for His purpose.
GORDON MACDONALD

❯❯ FOR FURTHER THOUGHT:

Where is your "line" when it comes to giving? Tithing? Donating a certain amount to charity? Giving until it hurts?

❯❯ PRACTICAL APPLICATION:

How can you stretch your limits when it comes to generosity?

I can't thank You enough, God, for the blessings You've given me. I don't want to be stingy with these blessings—reveal to me ways in which I can share each of my possessions with others.

EXCEED YOUR GRASP

But now they desire a better country—that is, a heavenly one. Therefore God is not ashamed to be called their God, for He has prepared a city for them.

HEBREWS 11:16

Some people accuse Christians of being so heavenly minded that they're no earthly good. That may be so at times, but it's also true that putting all your hope in this world does you no eternal good. The poet Robert Browning was on to something when he wrote, "A man's reach should exceed his grasp, or what's a heaven for?"

When Joseph and Mary found their twelve-year-old son in the temple, He told them, "How is it that you sought Me? Did you not know that I must be about My Father's business?" (Luke 2:49). Through the parable of the minas, Jesus told His followers, "Make a profit until I come" (Luke 19:13). In other words, God calls us to do everything with the ultimate goal of building His kingdom.

The full impact of your work on earth is measured not in material wealth but spiritual. How have you used what God has given you to see souls saved? That effort starts at home, extends through the church, and goes out into the world, always with the objective of seeing as many as possible arrive at the wonderful home God has for them.

But such a vision is only visible if you look beyond the cares of this world.

Paul had been shipwrecked, whipped, beaten,
stoned, and imprisoned. Throughout everything,
his faith enabled him to maintain perspective.
He realized that as long as he was doing what
he was supposed to do, his being labeled a success
or failure by others really didn't matter.
JOHN MAXWELL

✦ FOR FURTHER THOUGHT:

How might a truly heavenly perspective increase your productivity here on earth?

✦ PRACTICAL APPLICATION:

Make a list of every activity you do today. Then, before you go to sleep, go through the list and see how many of the items have eternal significance.

Lord, I know You've called me to make an impact
on earth while keeping my eyes fixed on eternity.
Teach me how to walk this delicate balance, giving
the maximum amount of glory to Your name.

WHERE DO YOU TURN FOR HELP?

God is our refuge and strength, a very present help in trouble. Therefore we will not fear, though the earth is removed, and though the mountains are carried into the midst of the sea, though its waters roar and are troubled, though the mountains shake with its swelling.

PSALM 46:1–3

When was the last time your life was disrupted? Do you fear future calamities? The psalm writer provides a picture of global cataclysms, natural disasters that would cause the strongest man's courage to melt. While the earth shakes, traditional sources of comfort and trust fall to pieces, and new threats emerge, God remains ever-present to help.

There is no condemnation for reacting to troubling situations with fear. . .but fear isn't the place to remain. The difference is where you turn. Do you look for comfort, strength, or protection in the world around you—in a stocked bank account or an escape into fantasy? Well, the appropriate response is a resolution to trust in the strength of God.

God is present in His beloved creation, and He is with you, His beloved child. He will not abandon you. Every other source of comfort and protection will dissipate, crumble, or slip away. Only God remains.

Since God Himself is a steadfast Rock, the foundation of all certitude and steadfastness, it must be by faith or holding fast to God that man can become steadfast.
ANDREW MURRAY

❯ FOR FURTHER THOUGHT:

Does turbulence in your physical life tend to impact the steadiness of your spiritual life? How so?

❯ PRACTICAL APPLICATION:

To prepare for the big trials of life, we must first master reacting well to the small ones. The next time an inconvenience crops up, practice handing the situation over to God—immediately.

Almighty God, You call me to rely on Your strength, so here I am, surrendering all my problems to You. Please take the wheel and steer my life back to where it needs to be.

CALLED TO FRIENDSHIP

And not only so, but we also rejoice in God
through our Lord Jesus Christ, by whom
we have now received the atonement.

ROMANS 5:11

Have you ever thought of yourself as a friend of God? If so, have you ever said it aloud?

True, the Bible doesn't talk often about this. Mostly, it's reserved for the great patriarch, Abraham, who is called God's "friend" in 2 Chronicles 20:7, Isaiah 41:8, and James 2:23. Another important early patriarch of the faith, Job, talks about his friendship with God in Job 29:4.

Then again, James 4:4 and Romans 5:11 make it clear that any man can be a friend of God if he repents, trusts Jesus Christ, and loves the Lord wholeheartedly.

By now, you may be thinking, *That's right. I'm a friend of God!* Do you believe it enough to say it aloud? Say it first in prayer to God. Then mention it in a conversation with your wife, child, friend, colleague, or neighbor. Why not try to create some other friends of God?

Our intimacy with God—His highest priority for our lives—determines the impact of our lives.
CHARLES STANLEY

❖ FOR FURTHER THOUGHT:

When was the last time you spoke with God not in formal prayer but in a heartfelt conversation?

❖ PRACTICAL APPLICATION:

How can you use your prayer life to truly live up to the title of "God's friend"?

Lord, I thank You for the opportunity to come to You in prayer. Teach me how to be less rigid and more open with You. I want our friendship to be more than mere words.

LOVE DOES NO HARM

Love works no ill to his neighbor;
therefore love is the fulfilling of the law.
ROMANS 13:10

The five books of Moses contained the law of God, and the overwhelming majority of these laws were intended to promote the well-being of the Israelites. Many of them were designed to bring about justice and restitution for those who had been wronged. They boiled down to this simple precept: do not harm your neighbor.

The apostle Paul explained that if you loved your neighbor, you'd automatically fulfill the law because you would avoid harming him. Thus, you should allow your life to be ruled by God's love. How? Simply by yielding to His Spirit. "God is love" and "the love of God has been poured out in our hearts by the Holy Spirit" (1 John 4:8; Romans 5:5).

Many men feel that they need to be rough and tough. We can't let anyone push us around. We need to be assertive in business dealings and never show weakness. Love and gentleness may seem wimpy by comparison.

But that's not true. You can be gentle to the weak, yet still be tough when you need to be. You can be assertive in business dealings, but adding love to the mix will make you honest and fair. You can act justly towards others without letting anyone push you around.

Answering God's call to love others takes courage and strength—it proves you're a true man of God.

Contrary to popular opinion,
it takes strength to be gentle.
LLOYD JOHN OGILVIE

❖ FOR FURTHER THOUGHT:

Go through the Ten Commandments and think of ways love fulfills each one.

❖ PRACTICAL APPLICATION:

How can you improve your love toward God and others? How can you make sure your behaviors are actively helping, and not hurting, other people?

Father, show me how to love others the way You want me to—not in a weak, sentimental way that may vanish tomorrow. I know that's the only way I can effectively fulfill Your calling.

TRANSFORMED BY REST

"Work shall be done six days, but the seventh day is the Sabbath of rest, a holy convocation. You shall do no work on it; it is the Sabbath of the LORD in all your dwellings."

LEVITICUS 23:3

Why did God command His people to set aside a specific day for rest? What do you think God could do in *your* life with one day set aside for rest?

Think about all the stuff that fills your calendar. Our countless obligations may include jobs and careers, caring for a family member, helping kids with schoolwork, or the chores and projects that pile up around the house. The question, "Why a Sabbath?" suddenly becomes, "Who has time for a Sabbath?"

The striking nature of God's call to rest may have a message for you today. What are you missing from God that could come from a weekly Sabbath? Perhaps a Sabbath offers an opportunity to place greater faith in God right now. Then again, it may be an opportunity to rely on others in your faith community. Regardless, the Sabbath is your chance to receive a blessing from God.

Sabbath, in the long run, is as essential
to your well-being as food and water,
and as good as a wood fire on a cold day.
MARK BUCHANAN

❯❯ FOR FURTHER THOUGHT:

Do you observe the Sabbath? If so, how?

❯❯ PRACTICAL APPLICATION:

What commitments can you either remove from your schedule, or at least shift to another day, to create a Sabbath rest in your life?

Teach me to rest, Father. I know You've called
me to work for You, but I can't make much of
an impact if all my strength is gone. I want to
do as much as possible to glorify Your name.

BE AN INTERCESSOR

I exhort therefore, first of all,
that supplications, prayers, intercessions,
and giving of thanks be made for all men.
1 TIMOTHY 2:1

After Moses received the Ten Commandments from God on Mount Sinai, he called the Israelites together and said to them, "The LORD talked with you face to face on the mountain out of the midst of the fire (I stood between the LORD and you at that time, to show you the word of the LORD, for you were afraid because of the fire and did not go up into the mountain)" (Deuteronomy 5:4–5). Moses often was the intermediary between God and His people. He interceded on their behalf.

Intercessory prayer is a divine act of love and service. It requires persistence, patience, and faith in God. Christians should intercede for family and friends, their country, government leaders, their pastors, the church, the poor, the sick, their community, their enemies, and especially for the unsaved. Wherever there is a need, God calls Christians to pray.

The Bible contains many examples of intercessory prayer. Look for them as you read the scriptures. Discover how God's people prayed and notice the great changes those prayers made.

Intercessory prayer is just as important today as it was in Moses' time. It draws believers nearer to God and provides them with a powerful way to help others. Whom will you pray for today?

When we hold up the life of another before God, when we expose it to God's love, when we pray. . .only then do we sense what it means to share in God's work, in his concern; only then do the walls that separate us from others go down and we sense that we are at bottom all knit together in a great and intimate family.
DOUGLAS STEERE

» FOR FURTHER THOUGHT:

Who do you know who needs some sort of physical or spiritual assistance that only God can provide?

» PRACTICAL APPLICATION:

Add that person (or those people) to your prayer list, and don't stop praying until the need is answered.

God, thank You for Your "front line" prayer warriors, many of whom have prayed for me when I really needed it. Help me return the favor and pray for them too—even the ones I'll never meet.

PRAYING WITH OTHERS

"O LORD, I implore You, let Your ear now be attentive to the prayer of Your servant and to the prayer of Your servants, who desire to fear Your name. And let Your servant prosper this day."

NEHEMIAH 1:11

Ezra and Nehemiah were contemporaries. In terms of their background, expertise, and leadership roles, the men hardly could have been more different. But in terms of their dedication to the Lord God, they both were all in. They stand out as two of the greatest men of prayer.

Before embarking on his journey from Babylon back to the promised land, Ezra gathered a great group of men together and proclaimed a fast. Then they humbled themselves before God and asked for a safe journey for themselves and their families (Ezra 8:21–23). A few months later, Ezra offered one of the Bible's greatest prayers of confession (Ezra 9:5–15).

Before asking the king's permission to leave his post and seek the welfare of his people, Nehemiah and other men prayed for four months (Nehemiah 1:4–2:1). While conversing with the king, Nehemiah shot up a bullet prayer (Nehemiah 2:4). Later, he and Ezra led another revival, which included another powerful prayer of confession—this time before all the people (Nehemiah 9:5–38).

Bottom line: Ezra and Nehemiah were champions of prayer. They always invited other men to join them in earnest, heartfelt, deep prayers. And they continued praying until they felt sure that God would answer.

How do you know when you're walking in the Spirit?
You know it when you're living a life of prayer,
because prayer is the proof of dependence on the Spirit.
TONY EVANS

⋙ FOR FURTHER THOUGHT:

Why do you think God values group prayer? What might the answer reveal about His attitudes toward community and human relationships?

⋙ PRACTICAL APPLICATION:

If you feel awkward praying in public, what small steps can you take to begin breaking that barrier?

Lord God, I don't want to always pray alone.
I know You've called me to something greater—
a community full of like-minded Christians
singularly seeking for Your will to be done.

A BEAUTIFUL THING

And being in Bethany in the house of Simon the leper, as He sat at the table, a woman came with an alabaster box of very precious ointment of spikenard. And she broke the box and poured it on His head. And there were some who had indignation within themselves and said, "Why was this waste of the ointment made? For it might have been sold for more than three hundred pence and have been given to the poor." And they murmured against her. And Jesus said, "Leave her alone. Why do you trouble her? She has worked a good work for Me. For you always have the poor with you, and you may do them good whenever you want. But you do not always have Me. She has done what she could. She has come beforehand to anoint My body for burial."

MARK 14:3–8

It is not possible to "waste" anything on Jesus if we are motivated by love. It's not a waste to give up our time, hopes, or valuables for the perfect future He offers. Others may scorn our gifts as impractical or impulsive, but Christ sees them as beautiful. In today's passage, the act of anointing a body that is still alive seems like nonsense, but it's the reason we know of this woman today (Mark 14:9).

We don't need to have great resources to do beautiful things either. This woman didn't occupy an important or powerful station in life, but as Jesus points out, she did what she could for Him. And she did it when the opportunity came, without hesitation and at the cost of scorn and criticism. God calls all of us to have the love and courage of that woman.

⌃

We hunger for beauty because it is a beautiful God whom we serve.
MICHAEL CARD

⇢ FOR FURTHER THOUGHT:

What is your idea of a "beautiful" life? How does this image fit with God's definition?

⇢ PRACTICAL APPLICATION:

Look for the beauty in your life today, even in the midst of monotony. Sprinkle your actions with kindness—a supportive word, a helping hand, etc.—and dwell on the ultimate purpose which God has called you to.

Thank You, God, for imbuing my life, which would otherwise be dull and insignificant, with the beauty of Your calling. I never want to overlook the marvelous in search of the mundane.

THE GOLDEN RULE

"Whatever you want men to do to you,
you should do just so to them."

MATTHEW 7:12

These words capture the essence of the Christian life—in every situation, God calls us to treat others as we ourselves want to be treated. This is indeed the "Golden Rule" of civilized humanity.

Tragically, the human heart is anything but golden. It is, in fact, deceitful above all things (Jeremiah 17:9) and therefore incapable—apart from God—of living by this rule. It rewrites the rule to say: "Do to others *before* they do to you," anticipating the betrayal of other hearts. It says, "Do to others as they *have* done to you," to justify the age-old maxim of retribution: "An eye for an eye, a tooth for a tooth."

But Solomon wrote, "Whoever digs a pit shall fall in it, and he who rolls a stone, it will return on him" (Proverbs 26:27). Any act of retribution will have its eventual payback: "God is not mocked, for whatever a man sows, that he shall also reap. For he who sows to his flesh shall of the flesh reap corruption, but he who sows to the Spirit shall of the Spirit reap life everlasting" (Galatians 6:7–8).

The Spirit enables us to obey the Golden Rule, so "let us not be weary in doing good, for in due season we shall reap, if we do not faint. Therefore, as we have opportunity, let us do good to all men, especially to those who are of the household of faith" (Galatians 6:9–10).

How do we define "good"? Apply the Golden Rule: what we think would be good for us, do the same for others.

If we can just understand that the Golden Rule way of living is the only correct method, and the only Christlike method, this will settle all of our difficulties that bother us.
GEORGE WASHINGTON CARVER

❯ FOR FURTHER THOUGHT:

Do you make a conscious effort to obey the Golden Rule each day? What does that look like on a moment by moment basis?

❯ PRACTICAL APPLICATION:

Think of areas of your life—work, family, friendships, the daily commute—that could use a better adherence to the Golden Rule. Then consciously put it into practice.

Father God, teach me how to live out Your Golden Rule in every action I take, every word I speak, and every interaction I have with others. I want to exemplify Your love to the entire world.

DISREGARD CONDEMNATION

*Who is he who condemns? It is Christ who died, yes,
rather, who was raised again, who is even at the right
hand of God, who also makes intercession for us.*

ROMANS 8:34

When Jesus Christ died on the cross, He paid the price
for our sins. When He rose from the dead, He broke the
power of death in our lives. If that wasn't enough, now that
He's sitting at the right hand of the Father in heaven, He
constantly intercedes for us.

So who's left to condemn us? The devil, of course. He's
called "the accuser of our brothers" (Revelation 12:10–11),
and he snipes at Christians before God day and night.
But we can overcome him with the blood of Jesus Christ—
the same blood that paid the price for our sin.

People sometimes condemn us, but the apostle Paul
said that we shouldn't pay attention to them (1 Corinthians
4:3). And we in turn are commanded not to judge others
(Matthew 7:1).

We often condemn ourselves, but even "if our heart
condemns us, God is greater than our heart" (1 John 3:20).

*It is easier to walk in triumph every day
when we know that the condemnation is
gone and that we're free to live in victory.*
BOB MOOREHEAD

❯❯ FOR FURTHER THOUGHT:

Why do you sometimes feel condemned? How effective was Jesus' work on the cross?

❯❯ PRACTICAL APPLICATION:

One of the devil's greatest tools is our own past. Think of some of the greatest Christian men throughout history—then consider their pre-Christian lives. How might their examples provide encouragement when your memories come back to haunt you?

---

*Thank You, Lord, for burying the past. I know
the old me is dead and gone, so I have no right
to try to bring him up again. Show me how to
walk in the new life to which You've called me.*

CALLED TO HUMILITY

Behold, how good and how pleasant it is
for brothers to dwell together in unity!
PSALM 133:1

In the very middle of his letter to the Ephesian church, Paul told the believers to be humble and diligent to preserve the unity of the Spirit (Ephesians 4:2–3). Unity of heart and mind among Christians is based on Christlike humility (Philippians 2:1–11).

When Christians argue and bicker and fight, what's the problem? Pride. One of the signs of pride is contempt—the attitude of "I'm right; you're wrong."

Respect is the opposite of contempt. Respect embraces the truth that everyone—your enemies, your brothers in Christ, and especially your church leaders—is made in the image of God. Great authority comes from great humility.

Another expression of pride is being judgmental and overly critical, as if you somehow know the motives of someone else's heart. Being nonjudgmental means assuming the best about the other person.

What is the difference between criticism and exhortation? Criticism seeks only to spotlight flaws. Exhortation comes from a heart of love with a desire to help the other person and walk alongside them awhile. When you speak into difficult situations, you restore others gently (Galatians 6:1–5).

Humility is healing. It alone releases the power and blessing of God among believers.

*Every human being is worthy of respect just
because we are created in the image of God.*
GARY AND MONA SHRIVER

❯❯ FOR FURTHER THOUGHT:

When others show you respect, are you encouraged?
How often do you return the favor?

❯❯ PRACTICAL APPLICATION:

Find ways to show respect to those around you
today: Tell your pastor that you appreciate his leadership. Show your wife how thankful you are for her.
Compliment a friend or coworker.

---

*Lord, it's sometimes easier to find fault
than it is to show respect. Teach me how
to take the better path each chance I get.*

ACCURATE WEIGHTS

A false balance is an abomination to the LORD,
but a just weight is His delight.

PROVERBS 11:1

An ancient commercial practice that scripture refers to often is the use of stones in making measurements.

Deuteronomy 25:13–14 says, "You shall not have in your bag differing weights, a great and a small. You shall not have in your house differing measures, a great and a small." Hosea 12:7 says, "He is a merchant. The balances of deceit are in his hand; he loves to oppress." And Proverbs 16:11 as well as Proverbs 20:10 address this issue of unbalanced scales and unjust weights.

In today's world, these biblical warnings would apply to the supermarket deli. Say you were purchasing two pounds of roast beef and assumed the meat on the scale was indeed the amount you requested. But when the next person in line placed the same order, the deli employee adjusted the scales and gave the person much more meat for the same price.

You would be understandably upset over such thing. So is God. He detests shady business practices. Because God is just, He takes the side of those who are treated unfairly. As you head to your work today, consider all of your own business practices. Are they fair and just?

Honesty is not so much a credit as an
absolute prerequisite to efficient service to
the public. Unless a man is honest we have
no right to keep him in public life.
THEODORE ROOSEVELT

›› FOR FURTHER THOUGHT:

What are some ways today's verse applies to modern
business practices and personal interactions?

›› PRACTICAL APPLICATION:

How can you speak up for yourself when you sense
you've been cheated? How can you speak up for
others?

Lord, I hate being cheated—so I never want
to inflict that emotion on somebody else.
Teach me how to take the honest route, even
when dishonesty looks easy and attractive.

A LEADER'S LIFE

*And when [Paul and Barnabas] had ordained
elders for them in every church, and had
prayed with fasting, they commended them
to the Lord in whom they believed.*

ACTS 14:23

Before their first missionary journey, Barnabas and Paul and other gifted men had been worshipping God, praying, and fasting. Now, near the end of that missionary journey, Paul and Barnabas were doing the same with the men they'd appointed as elders in each city.

What a great way for these converts to step into servant-leader roles within each city church. It's one thing to give your life to Jesus Christ; it's quite another to have dedicated, godly men join you in committing your relationship with the Lord. This causes you to sink your roots down deeper than ever.

True, not all Christian men will be appointed as leaders within the local church. Just the same, all should aspire to live up to the qualifications of such leaders (as spelled out in 1 Timothy 3:1–7; Titus 1:5–9; and 1 Peter 5:1–4).

The bottom line: Don't worry about whether you'll ever be appointed as a leader. God calls you to live as one just the same!

If you long to become a hero by acting heroically,
I personally know of no better way to accomplish
that task than to be a hero at home. How?
Work hard each day at becoming a servant
leader in your home. Honor your wife. Interact
with your children at a deep level. And commit
yourself to great character and integrity.
PAUL PETTIT

❯❯ FOR FURTHER THOUGHT:

Do you regularly do things in private that would
tarnish your witness for Christ if others found out?

❯❯ PRACTICAL APPLICATION:

Start thinking of yourself as a leader today. Remind
yourself of all the people who might see you as an
influence—and behave accordingly.

Lord, I thank You for giving me the opportunity
to be Your witness to this world. Help me live
up to Your high calling—for my sake and
for the sake of everyone who might see.

CALLED TO DISCIPLESHIP

As you have therefore received Christ Jesus the
Lord, so walk in Him, rooted and built up in
Him, and established in the faith, as you have
been taught, abounding in it with thanksgiving.
COLOSSIANS 2:6–7

How do we live as disciples of Christ? This verse gives us four simple guidelines to follow.

First, we reach out to Jesus in daily prayer, as He is now living within our hearts. Living with someone means spending time together so that we can learn His ways.

Second, we nourish our roots. Mighty trees have deep roots to support them in turbulent winds and terrible storms. Our roots are nourished with the waters of prayer and Bible study. This stabilizes us to face the storms in life.

Next, we draw strength by remembering what we've learned in the past and what we've been taught by others. Their words and examples fortify our faith.

Finally, we give thanks in all circumstances. Gratitude flows easily during good times, but even in difficult circumstances, expressing appreciation renews our spirits.

How do we live for God? By letting Him guide our lives through prayer and study, fellowship with others, and perpetual gratitude.

There is an old saying: Champions don't become champions in the ring—they are merely recognized there. That's true. If you want to see where someone develops into a champion, look at his daily routine.
JOHN MAXWELL

>> FOR FURTHER THOUGHT:

How have you specifically applied (or failed to apply) each of the four paths of discipleship in today's verse over the last few days?

>> PRACTICAL APPLICATION:

How can you improve your adherence to these disciplines?

Lord, it's easy to coast by on the name "Christian" without doing anything. But You've called me to a more rigorous—yet vastly more fulfilling— life. Teach me how to be a perfect disciple.

WHO HAS GOD ENTRUSTED TO YOU?

But on the contrary. . .they saw that the gospel
of the uncircumcision was committed to me,
as the gospel of the circumcision was to Peter.

GALATIANS 2:7

When Paul realized that God had entrusted him with reaching the Gentiles, it couldn't have been easy for him. He expressed his feelings in Romans 9:2–5. His heart was with the Jews. "I could wish that I myself were accursed from Christ for my brothers, my countrymen according to the flesh," he wrote in verse 3. Galatians 2:8 explains how Paul reached this conclusion: "For He who worked effectually in Peter to the apostleship of the circumcision, the same was mighty in me toward the Gentiles."

Whom has God entrusted to you? Are you open to the possibility that He might lead you to reach people who don't look, talk, or think like you—no matter how burdened you might be for those who do?

All around us are people who are lost and separated from their heavenly Father, and we have a responsibility to tell them about Him.
BILLY GRAHAM

❯❯ FOR FURTHER THOUGHT:

Who do you know who needs Jesus—but whom you just don't have a desire to speak to?

❯❯ PRACTICAL APPLICATION:

Today, try to overcome the barriers of awkwardness and start making connections in order to lead that person to Christ.

Lord, I know You've called me to tell others about You. So give me the courage to step out of my comfort zone and reach the lost—no matter who they might be.

IF YOU CLAIM TO LOVE GOD. . .

*If a man says "I love God" and hates his brother, he is
a liar, for how can he who does not love his brother,
whom he has seen, love God, whom he has not seen?*

1 JOHN 4:20

This is the verse that risks making hypocrites of us all.
Who among us doesn't know someone we'd cross the road
to avoid? That person might be obnoxious, dishonest, a
troublemaker—but he's still loved by God, and the Lord
wants every soul brought home.

What about people begging on the street? Lots of them
may be con artists, so we preserve our dignity by walking past.
But some of them are in real need, and God values the saving
of even a con artist above your dignity. We should never
pass up opportunities to engage with these wayward souls.

Then there are the people who have actually hurt us—
those we once trusted and can never forgive for their betrayal.
They weren't born cruel and callous. They too were hurt, so
they inflict hurt. God calls *you* to break that chain, to replace
hurt with love.

It's a big task. . .and one we will never be able to live
up to in our own power. But we will be nearer to God for
having tried!

*All who have received grace should
learn to be gracious to others.*
WATCHMAN NEE

❯ FOR FURTHER THOUGHT:

Do your attitudes toward others match up with God's?
What evidence do you have to support your answer?

❯ PRACTICAL APPLICATION:

Love isn't a one-time act—it's a way of life, an attitude
that reveals itself with every action we take. How do
you overcome cynicism or apathy toward those who so
desperately need God's love?

---

*Lord God, You've called me to many things—
servitude, holiness, kindness, and so on. But
all these callings can be summed up with
one word: love. Teach me how to walk in
this calling—the highest calling of all.*

SCRIPTURE INDEX

GENESIS
2:15. 296
39:3. 76

EXODUS
23:5. 328

LEVITICUS
11:44. 202
11:45. 202
19:2. 202
19:18. . . . . 176, 222
20:7. 202
20:26. 186
23:3. 344

NUMBERS
9:18–19. 18
12:7–8. 44
18:22–23. 334

DEUTERONOMY
5:4–5. 346
6:5. 176
8:18. . . . . 38, 230
10:9. 164
11:18–19. 164
22:4. 328
25:13–14. 360
32:4. 126

Joshua

1:8. 215
14:9, 12. 214
21:44. 194

Judges

15:16. 154
15:18–19. 154

1 Samuel

9:21. 218
12:23. 302
16:7. 294
23:2. 132
23:4. 132
24:6–7. 264

2 Samuel

2:4–5. 168
6:14–15. 242
6:21. 242
9:3. 130

1 Kings

2:2. 226
2:3. 226
11:1. 226
11:4. 226
11:6. 258
18:18. 256
19:20. 34
22:8. 286

2 KINGS

2:9. 146
22:19. 28

1 CHRONICLES

9:11. 26
9:13. 26
14:10. 62
23:4–5. 234
25:1. 234

2 CHRONICLES

1:10. 102
7:11–12. 320
17:6. 98
20:21. 116
20:27–28. 116
21:20. 116
26:3, 5. 156

NEHEMIAH

1:11. 348

JOB

16:20–21. 310
23:10. 246
29:24. 180
31:1. 274

PSALMS

1:1. 284
16:11. 268
19:13. 318

30:5. 170
34:19. 208
41:1. 192
46:1–3. 340
46:10. 128
51:1–4. 144
51:10–12. 144
55:4–5. 136
55:17. 136
55:22. 136
65:3. 114
73:25. 268
73:25–26. 88
75:6–7. 150
86:11. 178
88:9. 118
94:4. 280
97:10. 182
105:43. 26
107:15. 234
113:3. 116
119:11. . . . . 48, 228
119:68. 126
119:97. 128
119:105. 36
119:165. 158
131:1–2. 70
133:1. 356
139:5–6. 272
139:23–24. 182
143:5. 128
143:5–6. 184

Proverbs

1:5. 124
4:18–19. 120
8:13. . . . . 140, 182
11:1. 360
11:13. 260
13:4. 296
16:3. 90
16:24. . . . . 160, 196
17:9. 222
17:14. 52
19:1. 54
23:5. 38
24:17–18. . . . . 50, 168
25:21–22. 316
26:27. 352
28:13. 314
29:7. 290
29:11. 212
30:25. 72

Ecclesiastes

2:11. 226
5:10. 8
7:8. 298
7:26. 258

Song of Solomon

2:11–12. 170

Isaiah

2:11. 66
28:13. 304

30:23. 92
40:28–29. 138
40:31. 138
53:3. 94
55:7. 134
55:8. 134

JEREMIAH
2:5. 126
7:22–23. 304
7:24. 304
29:11. 60

EZEKIEL
4:4–5. 108
22:30. 250
28:2. 248

DANIEL
1:17. 58

HOSEA
12:7. 358

JOEL
2:25. 300

JONAH
1:3. 244

MICAH
7:1–2, 6. 46
7:7. 46
7:8. 46

HABAKKUK

3:17–18. 266
3:19. 266

HAGGAI

1:6. 16
1:9. 16

ZECHARIAH

4:6. 64

MATTHEW

3:4. 30
5:23–24. 188
5:27–28. 172
5:37. 82
5:44. . . . . 194, 316
6:20. 282
6:21. 268
7:12. 352
8:22. 252
10:28. 132
10:38–39. 204
13:20–21. 298
18:21–22. 278
19:16. 306
19:20. 306
19:21. 306
19:25. 262
19:26. 262
20:30. 288
22:34–40. 176

22:40. 190
22:40. 194
25:15. 96
25:21. 150
25:40. 200

MARK

4:9. 224
9:24. 20
9:35. 282
12:29–31. 190
14:3–8. 350
14:38. 244

LUKE

2:49. 338
4:13. 322
6:23. 152
6:27–28. 276
11:8. 330
11:9. 330
12:29–31. 178
18:17. 56
19:13. 338
23:40–41. 106
23:42. 106
23:43. 106

JOHN

3:36. 314
10:10. 324
12:25–26. 238
16:33. 60

Acts

1:9–11... 112
4:36–37.. 216
5:41... 152
14:22.. 84
14:23.. 360
23:1... 32
24:16.. 32

Romans

2:4.. 148
5:3–4.. 68
5:5.. 344
5:11... 342
6:16... 230
8:28.. 22, 300
8:34... 354
9:3.. 366
10:2–3... 198
11:3–4... 104
12:9... 182
12:10.. 122
12:13.. 162
12:21.. 264
13:10.. 344
13:14.. 220
15:4... 208
15:7... 122

1 Corinthians

2:12... 40
10:13.. 244

10:31. 296
16:13–14. 12

2 CORINTHIANS
1:3–5. 210
5:6. 232
5:7. 112
8:11–12. 74
9:6. 174
12:9. . . . . 138, 240
12:10. . . . . 138, 240

GALATIANS
2:7. 366
2:8. 366
4:6–7. 110
5:13. 122
6:7. 80
6:7–8. 352
6:9. 80
6:9–10. 352

EPHESIANS
1:4. 202
2:1. 42
2:10. 96
3:20–21. 86
4:25. 236
4:26. 212
4:29. 332
6:10. 230
6:17. 228

PHILIPPIANS

2:12. 120
2:14–15. 22
3:8. 270
3:15. 308
3:20. 254
4:4. 24

COLOSSIANS

2:6–7. 364
3:12–13. 312

1 THESSALONIANS

4:11. 96
5:18. . . . . 22, 152

2 THESSALONIANS

3:3. 322

1 TIMOTHY

1:19. 314
2:1. 346
4:15. 128
5:8. 178
6:10. 8
6:17. 38

2 TIMOTHY

2:15. 7
2:23–24. 52
3:16–17. 36

TITUS

1:8. 162
3:14. 336

HEBREWS

4:12 . . . . 158, 228
4:16 334
10:24–25 122
11:10 254
11:16 . . . . 254, 338
13:7 308

JAMES

1:22 82
2:8 14
2:13 312
2:16 162
2:17 290
4:6 66
4:7 322
4:12 100
4:14 78
5:16 142

1 PETER

1:13–17 186
1:15–16 202
3:9 166
3:13–14 10
5:6 . . . . 66, 140

2 PETER

2:8 104

1 JOHN

1:9 314
3:20 354

4:8. 344
4:20. 368
4:20–21. 292
5:3. 304

2 JOHN
1:6. 206

JUDE
1:3. . . . . 52, 326

REVELATION
12:10–11. 356

MORE DEVOTIONS FOR MEN

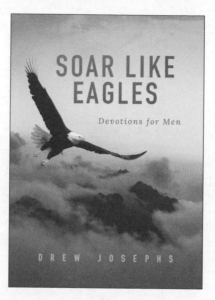

Isaiah 40:31 is a familiar and favorite scripture—and this
devotional will help you find the courage and strength it
promises by waiting on God. Through 120 entries, this book
will give you a powerful perspective on what it means to
"wait on the Lord" and how that benefits your life.

Paperback / ISBN 978-1-63609-555-4